SURVIVING

(The Only Option!)

JEANNETTE MEIJER

Ordering Information:

Books to Life Marketing Ltd
128 City Road, London, EC1V 2NX, UK

Printed in the United States of America

CONTENTS

How My Life Started
Chapter 1 / 1

The Separation
Chapter 2 / 6

With the Bible in the Hand
Chapter 3 / 11

Praise the Lord
Chapter 4 / 14

The Deterioration
Chapter 5 / 19

The Eviction
Chapter 6 / 24

On My Own Feet
Chapter 7 / 27

A New Start
Chapter 8 / 31

My years in Schiedam
Chapter 9 / 34

Back to the North
Chapter 10 / 39

A New Challenge
Chapter 11 / 44

Brussels...Belgium
Chapter 12 / 47

To Portugal
Chapter 13 / 52

Back to Holland
Chapter 14 / 59

A Positive Change
Chapter 15 / 62

The Big Step
Chapter 16 / 65

The New Life in Alkmaar
Chapter 17 / 69

Bad News
Chapter 18 / 71

The Answers to My Questions
Chapter 19 / 74

Finally See My Mother's Grave
Chapter 20 / 79

Present and Future
Chapter 21   / 82

Accept and Move On
Chapter 22   / 86

Sonja
Chapter 23   / 88

A New Way to Go
Chapter 24   / 94

Back to my Beloved Island, Crete
Chapter 25   / 99

TO ALL MY READERS

I dedicate this book to all the victims and the conquerors of (sexual) child abuse in the past or even still now. The inner strength is our most beautiful and precious possession.

To get forward in life you'll have to deal first with your past. The trauma's we've suffered will be there for the rest of our lives.

The biggest lost is that, what died in us while we were still alive.

My hope is that by writing this book I can help others in the process dealing with their dark past.

I will write about my bizarre and unbelievable story, even sometimes unbelievable for myself. Like it was only a bad dream.

Let me state that all children have the right to receive love, attention and warmth. A child also has the right of going to school, structure, food and playground.

I want to say to all of them to believe in the power to make the choice to become the conqueror and not the victim. Only you can make that choice. Nobody else can make that choice for you. Not an easy choice but if you want to have a future it is a very important choice. Don't give the abusers the satisfaction they took your life away from you.

There always will be this hole inside of you, as long as you live and nobody, nobody will be able to fill this hole. That feeling of loneliness will always be inside of you and you have to find a way to live with that.

At unexpected moments, the fear of the past comes back and I feel the pressure inside. My muscles get cramped, special if someone starts yelling at me. Then I can't get a word out of my mouth anymore and I turn inside myself. This kind of moments will never go away and you have to give it a place in your life. My story exposes the paradox of child abuse. No child is so loyal to their parents/guardians like an abused child, despite the injustice done to him. Abused children are always looking for the love of their parents/guardians.

To survive abuse, one must first break the taboo, which is very important. This is what I try to do by writing this book. The outside world prefers to look the other way through denial and shame rather pretend nothing has happened but if victims break this taboo without shame, without guilt then they can talk openly about the abuse. It's not your fault, don't blame yourself.

The penalty for silence is life imprisonment.

Hidden Things

From all I did and all I said,
Let no one try to find out who I was.
An obstacle was often there that changed the pattern
Of my actions and the manner of my life.
An obstacle was often there
To stop me when I'd begin to speak.
From my most unnoticed actions,
My most veiled writing _
From these alone will I be understood.
But maybe it isn't worth so much concern,
So much effort to discover who I really am.
Later, in a more perfect society,
Someone else made just like me
Is certain to appear and act freely.

—C.P. Cafavy.
Translated by Edmund Keely and
Philip Sherrard.

How My Life Started

THERE WAS THIS cute little house in a small village in the north of Holland. The name of this village is Nieuwe Schans. I was born in this little cute house and lived there with my mother, step-father and my two older half-sisters Gerda and Grietje. Gerda was the oldest, she was 9 years old, Grietje was 4 years old and I was 1 year and 4 months the day our whole lives would change.

My mother married my step-father when she was 20 years old (1947) and it was not at all a happy marriage. The reason for this marriage had nothing to do with love. All my mother wanted was a roof above her head and a man who could provide for her. My step-father was married before and that marriage lasted for only 9 months. No children came out of this marriage because he couldn't beget children. After the marriage with my mother his father came also to live with them until he died in 1955.

There was not much love in this marriage or better no love at all and there were many problems between them. My mother was a diffi-cult woman and she had slept with many men before the marriage. She saw no reason to stop this way of living once she got married. While my step-father was working all day, our house was a meeting point for international truckdrivers. Occasional she locked the old man up in the cellar so she would not be disturbed while she was doing what she was doing. My oldest half-sister was often sent out to look for men in the streets to take them home to my mother.

Also many times my mother left the house for a few days to go with a truckdriver on the road. We were left home alone with the old man and she didn't care. She abused us very often and locked my two sisters up when she found that necessary. I was a baby so I was not in the way. We didn't get much food and for sure not healthy food and I came never out of the house which caused a lack of vitamin D and I developed Rickets.

When my oldest half-sister was born everybody in the village were talking. Everybody knew what she was doing while my step-father was working but my mother didn't care and continued living her life with her hunger for sex.

My other half-sister was born and after I came (6-12-1956).

My step-father knew he was not our father but loved us anyway. He was a good man and his family didn't want to have anything to do with him because of all the shit he accepted from my mother.

Then the fatal day came, the day that would change all our lives 22th of April 1958.

My step-father came home from his work with the train around 17.30 hours. Probably my mother had been out all day so she had not prepared food. We were all in the kitchen and my step-father asked her why there was no food ready. I will never know what her answer was but for once he became angry cause there was no food for him but also not for us, the children. How ever he didn't want a big argument in front of the children and walked to the dresser, got the bread and a big knife to cut the bread in slices. My mother then said something nasty and something inside of him snapped. He had been hurt and humiliated too many times. In all his frustrations of the past years there was this fatal moment. He turned around and without a correct aim, he throws the knife at her and the knife went straight into my mother's heart...she felt down and died instantly. Me and my half-sisters witnessing this tragedy and we started to scream and were hysterical.

My step-father went outside to get a doctor but it was far to late. Police came and they took my step-father away. That was the last time we saw him. In a few seconds we've lost everything. In a few seconds our lives would never be the same again. Our mother was dead and our step-father in prison. We only had each other; three half-sisters, with three different fathers, without parents and without family because the parents of my mother and her sisters didn't want to know us because we were bastard children and they didn't want to have anything to do with us. As if you could blame us to be born. We didn't asked for all of this.

Also the family of my step-father didn't want anything to do with us cause they knew we were bastards and because of my mother's behaviour my step-father end up in prison.

What to do with the three girls, what to do with us? The first three weeks our neighbour mrs. Bisschop took us in and was taking care of us but we could not stay there forever. She had her own family to take care of and those three weeks were only to think of a solution what to do with us, the three orphans. They placed us in an orphanage. We were excluded by everyone and all we had was each other. We had three different fathers and I'm sure they didn't know about our existence.…how could they?

We were placed in an orphanage from the government and because there was no money they had to look after us in every way possible.

My mother's family didn't want to look after us and at the burial of my mother there was only one person present, a brother-in-law. They putted her in the ground without ceremony, without a headstone writing her name and the names of the children. Like she never existed.

Ok, she was what she was and many, many years later when I was searching for her grave and looking for the truth I found out why she was how she was and why she did the things she did. I then understood that she was like many others a victim of the war. We lived at the border with Germany and in the second world war her father, my grandfather did send her to the camp of the German soldiers, she was only around thirteen years old, and she only was allowed to go back home when she had coffee and tabaco for the family. You don't need a lot of imagination to understand what she had to do for her shopping list. In fact she was explored as a hooker by her own father, he made her a prostitute and later she didn't know better than being one.

I never met my grandparents and now I'm happy I haven't. Also I've never met the sisters of my mother. How they could have done this to my mother and later blame her. When I learned the truth I only could feel sorry for my mother.

My step-father was sent to prison for three years. He told everybody that once he would come out of prison he wanted the three of us children back with him. How noble of him because he knew he was not our biologic father.

They wanted to release him from prison after one and a half year but a few months before he would have been released he hung himself in his cel on 21st of august 1959. The reason I will never know but I can guess. Poor man who had only goodness inside of him. In this tragedy there were no winners, only losers. From this moment we were completely alone and at the mercy of strangers who pretended they wanted the best for us. Well, that I would learn fast and in the hard way but it made me the person I am now; combative, proud, ambitious and above all my love of liberty. The feeling of being all alone in this world is powerful and painful. When you realize that you don't belong anywhere, no bond with anyone, it makes you hard with readiness to fight. You don't have a choice realy.

The Separation

CHAPTER 2

MY FAMILY DIDN'T want us. They didn't want to know us so my sisters and me were placed in an orphanage and degraded to poor-relief. In the beginning we were not children who caused problems but one thing was sure; we had all three different characters which was normal because we all three had different fathers and we lived already a trauma.

My oldest sister suffered the most from this tragedy for she was nine years old and whiteness all that had happened. For her it was really hard to cope with all of it. She was the one who had to take men from the street and bring them home to our mother. She grew up with this task and didn't know better. For her it was normal behaviour so when we were placed in foster-care she brought men home because for her that was normal but the foster parents didn't accept this behaviour and she had to go back to the orphanage. She stayed there till she became eighteen years old and got married because she was pregnant. My other sister and me were not allowed to see her because the foster-parents and social workers shared the opinion that she was a bad example for us so they kept us separate. We were not allowed to have any contact with each other.

Grietje and me stayed in foster-care with a couple in the north of Holland in the city named Leeuwarden. This couple didn't have children and aged already. They were strong church- going people, rigid and we had to live with many rules. We were there on contract base. Adoption was never an option. My sister was in contrast with me, docile and the foster- parents loved her for that. They never had problems with her. I was something different, always asking questions, looking for answers and reasons but they did not accept discussions. Their motto was simple; just do what we tell you to do and everything is ok.

For me that didn't work because I was always looking for the how and the why. Looking for the truth. In material way we did fine. Of course they got payments for having us and they spend that money on us. Clothes, food and even musical education. I went to music school learning to play the flute. Yes, in material way we were fine but what is that worth if you were not allowed to talk about your feelings? When I was about seven/ eight years old I became more and more conscious about many things in my life. I am an emotional person and I wanted to talk about the things that kept me busy, my past for example. But talking about the past was not allowed, not done.

They waved everything away with the argument that they were now my parents and that was the only thing that counted. For me this was unacceptable of course because I needed answers to all the questions in my head. I needed to know the truth. I was a baby when the tragic dead of my mother took place so I did not have memories about all that. My foster-parents told me that my parents died in a car-crash but I knew instinctive that that was a big lie. If that was the truth why they were so mysterious about it. Why I was not allowed to talk about it? I was like a pittbull, my teeth where in it and I was determined to get the truth on the table.

I didn't know then that the truth would come to me many, many years later.

My foster-parents explained my determination as bold, ungrateful and rebel. I felt more and more unhappy and lonely and the only way to express my feelings was in music. I romanticised my mother. I didn't know her, didn't know how she looked like, her voice, her smell.... I knew nothing about her and same thing with my father. Who was he. Did I look like my mother, or like my father? My sister had curly, dark hair with blue eyes. I had blond, style hair and brown eyes, so I wondered how my mother would have looked like. I didn't know anything, didn't have a photo so I made an image in my head. Maybe strange to understand but I missed her although I didn't know her. I felt lonely and misunderstood. I was lucky to have my music and playing the flute, a beautiful instrument, my singing, listening to music and I even wrote songs in English as good as I knew how to do that.

One of the songs I wrote:

Times

Tears are coming, tears are going
That's a thing that never ends
But the wind comes and starts blowing
With happiness in both his hands
Times of laughing, times of crying
And you think that nobody cares
Only one, but they were lying
And there are things you cannot bare
Times of needing, times of wanting
You can't get it, it's far away
You look for it, search for something
What that is you cannot say
Times of loosing, times of finding
And you think you've found your way
It's the wrong one cause you're hiding
But life goes on, yes, everyday.

I wrote this poem when I was about eleven years old. It shows how much I was struggling with my feelings. I could only express myself on paper for there was nobody to talk with about my feelings.

I remember a Sunday in summer. We had been to church which was always a battle for me. Manny Sundays we had to go two times to church and in between Sunday school for bible study. That Sunday we were sitting at the table for some lunch and my foster-mom made that day this horrible soup from which she knew I could not eat it, it was horrible for me. Only the smell made me almost throw up. Everybody started to eat except me. I could not. I saw the angry look of my foster-father and I knew that didn't promised any good. After staring at my plate for 5 minutes he said to me: "When your plate is not finished in five minutes I kick you upstairs". The silents that followed was threaten so I had to think of something fast. After two minutes I stood up from the table, walked towards the door and said to him: "I can manage to walk upstairs by myself". Same time I started to run and of course he came behind me, grabbed a wooden cloth-hanger from the row of pegs in the hall and started to hit me with it. Believe me, that was not a nice feeling. I had to stay the rest of the day in my room and again I felt very lonely and I thought I would be better of dead. In the bathroom I found aspirin and thought one strip would be enough to do the job. I started to eat them but after a while I became nauseas and got stomach-ache. I threw up and I knew this wouldn't work and life continued. At school I was a good student and I enjoyed learning things. Specially languages.

My foster-parents didn't know how to give compliments and we never did well enough, other children did always better. We also had to be very grateful for all the opportunities we were offered. As I told before, the word "gratitude" was the keyword and if something didn't go their way, we were immediately accused of ingratitude.

Sometimes we were locked up in a closet and they threatened to send us back to the orphanage if we would not obey. My foster-father was a police reserve and this fact was also regularly used in suppression. Just do as we say or else....

With my sister this worked perfectly but with me it was another story. The power-struggle between my foster-father and me got bigger and bigger and trust me, not because I wanted that, quite the opposite, but he wanted to get me down, humiliate me and show his power over me and that was not an easy job for him because I was very smart for my age.

This man didn't realized that by talking with me he would achieve much more but these people had very wrong views on parenting and therefor I never understood why they were eligible to take in foster children. They lived with an ostrich policy rarely seen anymore. Their opinion was the only right one and what they did not want to see, was not there in the first place. That was their way of living.

With the Bible in the Hand

MY FOSTER-PARENTS WERE strictly reformed so the bible quotes were flying around your ears with great regularity. The dear Lord was called into everything.

My foster-father in particular was a strict believer and, as usually the case with strict believers, with the bible in the hand, everything was justifiable.

On Sundays we were not allowed to play outside. We went to church twice every Sunday and in between to Sunday school. I hated Sundays, the long sitting on those hard wooden pews and long sermons that I didn't understand anything about it.

The only thing I did like was the singing together because I was into music. Half an hour before the service started we were already sitting there and to pass the time I was counting the hats of the ladies. I was so bored. My foster-father was an elder and of course sat in front with the other elders next to the pulpit. How proud he was. Prestige was so important to this man. To the outside world he was acting perfectly and my foster-mom of course played the act along. They made everybody think they had adopted us with the goodness of their heart but that was a big lie. On all my diploma's from schools my last name was theirs which was legally of course not true. That was not legitimate at all. Inconvenient for me also later in my life because at job applications I naturally had to explain this. These people only thought about themselves and what the consequences were for me was not important.

They gained their prestige through trickery and deceit. When I became little older my foster-father became sexually interested in me which for many readers will not come as a surprise I guess. It went subtle and sophisticated, but slowly it happened. I did not speak about it of course, because, who would believe me? Me, an orphan, living of the goodness of this God-fearing, hard working-man. A respectable member of the church, reserve in the police-force...no, one would say I was making it up.

But it happened anyway.

My sister was not bothered by him and maybe it was also to assert his power that way towards me. It all started around my ninth year, subtly in the car as we drove to the post-office in the evening to take away the post of that day work which had to be done before 7 pm in the evening. My sister never had to come with him, only me. It started with tentative groping and stayed there for a while. I guess he was testing me so see if I would talk. I didn't. I didn't dare to talk to anybody about this. I started to become painfully aware of my sexuality. He never really penetrate me but let do other sexual games with him. At that age, I already looked pretty feminine and that didn't really help. The feeling of loneliness and isolation was only increased by this new situation. I became increasingly unruly and resisted everything and everyone. It was my way of dealing with it. I was confused and did not know how to deal with all of this.

I was lonely now in this new relation with my foster-father. It was not a relation that support, protect or offering a safe home but a relation that exploit and isolate. I was alone, with this incomprehensible experiences. I was also afraid that everyone could see where my body was used for. I felt I was not worth being protected. Maybe I was not normal and do I understand everything wrong. Maybe I am over sensitive, exellerating what happens to me and maybe I find myself to important. I felt like I was worth nothing, not understood and withdrew into myself and my music.

NOTE:

Surely it is not up to children to show understanding for their parents or foster parents? Besides, I was far too unhappy. I could only rebel against their way of parenting; the unspoken things, I have no attachment, no bond, no structure. I learned to save myself by arming myself. I raised myself with what was at hand, as best as I could.

Praise the Lord

MY FOSTER-FATHER WAS a food representative by profession and his working area was in the north of Holland. He daily visited his regular customers, mostly grocers. One of his customers lived in our hometown named Leeuwarden and this customer had a grocery shop and a mobile grocery shop. His name was Mr. Ploeg. His shop was close to the music school where I took music lessons. Mr. Ploeg was also a musician and like me he also played in a brass band with the name "praise the Lord" (looft den Heer). Like my foster-father he also was an elder in the church. Two of his children, a boy and a girl, were also playing in the brass band and were sitting next to me. The daughter was playing the piccolo and the son the clarinet. I played the flute. Because of Mr. Ploeg I had joined the band.

Music was my life and even though the name of the band displeased me, I did love the participation in it. We played beautiful parts like Orpheus in the underworld and I had a lot of fun playing in this orchestra. I did very well if I do say so myself.

However, during the rehearsals I did notice that Mr. Ploeg looked at me a lot and smiled at me constantly. He played the drums and cymbals and stood somewhere at the back of the little hall where we rehearsed, right next to the entrance.

Whenever I had to go to the toilet, he often came behind me, start groping and kissing me. I hated it but didn't say anything.

He was a client of my foster-father and a good friend and so it was two against me. I was about twelve years old and not up to it. I kept my mouth shut and silently endured my faith. What else could I do? I hardly dared to go to toilet because I knew he would follow and then those nasty things happened.

My foster-father and Mr. Ploeg were of course in regular contact because they were business associates. One day Mr. Ploeg told my foster-father that there were diploma's to be obtained for me namely diploma's A, B and C for brass band.

He said that of course I would need some extra tutoring and that he was willing to take that on. Between these two men that was settled. The exams for diploma A were already in two months so tutoring had to start soon. When I was told all this, my anxiety became even greater but I had no say in this.

The first tutoring session was fixed and Mr. Ploeg would pick me up at home and bring me back home after the lesson. This was of course much appreciated by my foster-parents. I'm sure my foster-father knew exactly what was going to happen. I was handed to Mr. Ploeg on a silver platter. As soon as I was in his car (Mercedes) he started, while driving, kneading my small breasts with his fat sausage fingers, so hard that it hurt and just as hard he also squeezed my nipples. I was horrified but dared not say anything. Every time I went through hell. This was another big secret and couldn't talk to anyone about it. He was a client of my foster-father and for sure partner in crime.

As he understood after a few times, I was not going to talk he became bolder each time and went one step further and further. Then one evening he picked me up again for tutoring and to my great surprise I noticed he was driving out of town and thus not to tutoring session. During the ride, he was kneading my breasts painfully again and apart from the pain I felt this fear of what was in store for me, fear for the unknown.

After driving for about half an hour we arrived at a campsite. It was February and in the sky there was a full moon lightening up the evening and it was cold. He parked the car next to a caravan and turned off the engine. I was so afraid of what was to come.

First, we stayed in the car for a bit and he groped me extensively. He also started kissing me and penetrated my mouth with his tongue. Soft moans came out of his throat and his voice became hoarse. His thick sausage fingers disappeared into my underwear and I stiffened with fear. I was so afraid and knew there was nothing I could do to escape from this situation. Eventually, he made me get out of the car and he opened the door of the caravan. We went inside and he ordered me to take my clothes off and to go lie on the bed. I was terribly cold but did what he ordered me to do. I was at the mercy of this terrible man and couldn't go anywhere. I also didn't know where I was, in the middle of nowhere.

The moonlight shone faintly in the caravan and so I could see him undressing, smiling at me as he came to lie beside me on the bed. He took off his glasses and a saw a twinkle in his eyes.

Again he started groping my body and I felt his penis getting hard. At one point he grabbed something and did something with his penis. I understood that this must have been a condom. Then he lay on top of me with his heavy, fat body and panting heavily and raped me that night in his caravan. The image of his pudgy face above me while he raped me and had his orgasm I will never forget. To this day those images recur in my dreams. His breathing heavy, his voice hoarse. I smelled his sweat as his tongue slid across my lips and neck and I got nauseous and felt like choking.

After he finished, he smiled at me faintly and asked me if I had enjoyed it. I started crying softly and was happy to get dressed again. Without exchanging another word, we got back in the car and he took me back home. Two streets before we got home, he told me this was our little secret and not to talk to anyone about it. I said nothing. The abuse succeeded and binding me to him he trapped me, he had the power. He controlled me, my body and my mind. My thoughts, my mixed feelings were about him, our relation. I was trapped.

I had no words, nor was I looking for them. I was completely empty inside. He dropped me off at home, talked and laughed a little while with my foster-father and then drove off. I lied to my foster-mom about how the tutoring had gone and then quickly went to my room. I wanted to be alone, to reflect on this terrible night. My whole body ached, my breasts, between my legs, everywhere I had pain. When I undressed for the second time that evening, I saw blood in my underwear. I wrapped it in a peace of paper to throw it away the next day. I got in to my bed and suddenly tears steamed down my cheeks; I couldn't stop. I felt so much pain and sadness coming to the surface and the worst part was that I could not talk to anyone about it.

This man had also taken my body. My body...yes, but my head... never! My head remains mine alone!!!!

That night I didn't sleep a wink. With burning eyes I lay in my bed and stared into the darkness. It hurt, so terribly much pain and again I couldn't hold back my tears.

NOTE:

I blame her, her silence. I blame her for letting these men have their way. I blame her for not fighting for me, for watching me psychologically destroy myself, for not doing anything to understand me.

In fact I was like a stray dog with a lack of love. I was in dire need of my feeder manager of caressing gestures and my kennel of affection. I wanted so badly for them to love me!

Adult Child

The child who is not allowed to be a child.
No carefree time.
No laughing with friends.
A feeling of loneliness.
Not really understood by anyone.
A heart filled with pain.
How wonderful it would be
Just to be a child.
No difficult thoughts
No worries in your head.
A loving parent,
Who really believes in you.
Please, let me be a child,
Carefree and with a smile.
Enjoy being young,
Rejoice in a new day.
Yvonne Schotanus.
(thank you)

The Deterioration

SEVERAL TIMES I have been back in that caravan only to be raped again and again. I didn't dare say any one because I was afraid no one would believe me. I also had a kind of feeling of shame. I felt guilty for letting him have his way even though I hated it.

Only when I passed two exams and passed both diploma's A and B, I no longer had to go to the tutoring sessions and Mr. Ploeg could no longer abuse me.

At school I was not doing so well anymore, I could not concentrate anymore. I was confused and felt different from the other girls at school. I felt I didn't belong anywhere because I was so much more mature than the girls my age. I was also walking around with a big secret that I couldn't say anything about of course.

Grietje, my half-sister was no use to me either because we differed too much in everything and didn't have a close band together. She had left school at a young age and was working in a shop. She had a courtship and when she was seventeen she married this boy and left the foster home and me. I was left alone. I guess it was her way out of the foster home and its regime.

I was fourteen at the time and the situation was not getting any better. I still went to school but played truant a lot. A girl from my class once took me to see an older friend of hers who had an eyewear shop near our school. His name was Dirk-Jan.

Dirk-Jan became also my friend. He was kind, understanding, had a listening ear and didn't treat me like an unwed child. I visited him almost every day for a coffee, sometimes alone, sometimes with the girl from my class. Dirk-Jan became important to me because he was the only person who really listened to me and the only person who understood my situation within the foster-family. He took me seriously. I never told him about the sexual abuse cause I kept that secret deep inside of me.

On a certain day, it was school holiday, I had visited my oldest half-sister secretly and she had given me a photograph showing my mother and step-father on their wedding day. It was in black and white. That was the first time I saw my mother's face. My half-sister didn't tell me that the man in the picture was my step-father. She said it was our father and I believed her of course. How could I know different? I was allowed to borrow it to have a copy made. I took the photo to Dirk-Jan cause I knew he would help me with this. After one week waiting, the photo was ready and Dirk-Jan had enlarged it beautifully. Now finally I had a photo of my parents. I kept studying their faces and couldn't get enough of watching the photo. Specially I studied my mother's face. One thing I couldn't place and that was the fact she had dark, almost black curly hair, so different then my hair.

I had made a "thank you" card for Dirk-Jan and in it I also asked him to describe me. His opinion was very important to me and I felt very insecure. A while later I got a note back from him and he wrote:

Dearest Janna, thank you for your post. You asked me if I would describe you. Dearest Janna, I believe I could not. You are so unique that anything I would write about you would only be a dull reflection of reality. Never, no never could I forget you. You are very and actually far too wise for your age.

The tragedy of this is that you never enjoy life like any other girl of this age would. I hope I live long enough for you to make up for this loss you now have to go through, one day. Unfortunately he is no longer with us, but regularly I think of him and what he meant to me in those difficult years. With him I had a voice and I was grateful for that.

I was very happy with the photo and at that moment I could not have guessed that this photo would turn my life completely upside down. I decided to hang the picture on the wall in my little room above my bed so that I could always look at it. However, when my foster-parents saw the photo hanging on the wall they became so angry with me. I didn't understand what I had done wrong and didn't understand their anger. Why could they not be happy for me? I knew it was forbidden to talk about my parents but why could I not have a picture of them? Isn't it normal to have a photo of your parents?

Tensions were mounting and I felt more and more misunderstood and unloved. My foster-parents refused to understand me and wouldn't listen to me at all. My opinion and my feelings were totally unimportant to them. I refused to go to church with them anymore and the fights escalated. I had dropped out of school in the third grade and I wanted to look for a job so I did. I applied for a function at a bank (ABN- bank) and got the job. I was hired and went to work in the securities department. As I was only fifteen years old I was not allowed to work five days a week but only four days. I had to go to some special school for one day a week. I had a nice job and that one day school was fun too. I could choose from three handicraft classes every week. Woodworking, modelling or basket weaving.... So cool.

My foster-parents were anything but happy with me and behind my back they had contacted the child protection board. The social worker's report said the following:

Foster-father called me. There were problems with Janna. I made an appointment for the 6th of December, the birthday of Janna. (I only realized this later). Janna was not home because she had been sent away to her sister's house. The problems came down to Janna not acting the way foster-parents wanted.

Moreover they found it strange that she had a picture of her own parents hanging in her room. Janna was struggling with identification problems and could not talking to her foster- parents about it. Foster-parents were very disappointed in her and soon talked about out-of-home-placement. Janna herself did not want this at the time. She tried to make of it what she could. Since the first meeting on the 6th of December, meetings had taken place every fortnight, with the foster-parents together and with Janna separately.

Pretty soon, foster-father stopped interfering. He was too busy with his work and made it clear that he thought it was all nonsense. Now if only Janna did what foster-parents wanted, all problems would be solved.

Janna appreciated the conversations with me and she clearly expressed that she felt I was trying to understand her. However the situation only worsened. Conversations with foster-mother were an endless litany of complaints and aggression. Although I always tried to avoid becoming partisan, by the end it was almost impossible for me, to feel connected to Janna.

Clear words in this report of the social worker. I felt so unwanted and did not understand why. What had I done to them? I wanted their approval so badly but I had failed them so much.

NOTE:

I want to be born again, start over because it seemed to me that I had fallen into a nightmare. I knew my life wasn't normal because I could see that in girlfriends. They were protected by their mothers, brothers and sisters. It was taken away from me but now I want to be free, I want to live and find myself again.

Candles

The days of the future stand in front of us
Like a line of candles all alight....
Golden and warm and lively little candles.
The days that are past are left behind,
A mournful row of candles that are our;
The nearer ones are still smoking,
Candles cold, and melted, candles bent,
I don't want to see them: their shapes hurt me.
It hurts me to remember the light of them at first.
I look before me at my lighted candles,
I don't want to turn around and see the horror
How quickly the dark line is lengthening,
How quickly the candles multiply that have been put out.

—Constantine P. Cavafy

The Eviction

CHAPTER 6

JUST IMAGINE.

The fact that I had a picture of my parents hanging on the wall of my bedroom my foster-father called "difficulty". Who had difficulties? Did these people understand nothing at all and why were they so terribly self-ish? It never occurred to them for a moment that it was precisely their support I needed, their understanding, their help. For what reason had they taken me in as foster-child? With these people, my well-being did not come first, only their own ego. What I felt or thought was totally irrelevant and therefor not considered. Still I kept fighting desperately for some love, acceptance and approval from them. Unfortunately for noth-ing because I was remained the black sheep. These people left a big mark on me, a mark that I still suffer from to this day. There was no turning the tide, because they were simply hostile towards me. Luckily I had my job at the bank but at home I couldn't do anything right at all. Discussions regularly took place with the social worker and she recognized that the situation was not untenable anymore. The social worker asked me what I wanted, either to another foster home or to an orphanage till the age of eighteen. I let her know that I had other plans for myself. I wanted to take care of myself, find a room and live on my own. She thought I was to young for that but promised me to discuss it. The situation at home became untenable and I had to leave as soon as possible. The social worker wrote the following in her report:

The foster-parents issued an ultimatum: Janna had to leave within fourteen days, to where they did not care. Although I was a bit hesitant about rooming in the beginning, I did have confidence in Janna, she showed more and more independence and, in my opinion, was capable of taking care of herself. Janna soon found a room and together one Saturday, we bought all kind of things and decorated the room. She was happy.

Yes, on the one hand I was happy to be rid of the fights, intimidations and the abuse but at the same time I was also very sad and lonely. I felt unwanted and rejected and did not understand what I had done so wrong to these people.

The room I found was very small, maybe 35m2. It barely fitted a bed, a wooden box as table, two wooden boxes as a cup board and a rattan chair.

My foster-parents didn't let me much to take with me, so I didn't needed so much space. I had to leave behind things that were actually mine, such as dolls and games etc. like gifts given on birthdays. They gave me some clothes to take and that was it.

The day came when I left for good. I will never forget that evening. My foster-parents brought me by car and dropped me off at the door, no goodbyes, no encouraging words.... nothing. I went inside my new home and sat down on the bed, bewildered. I stared ahead and it wasn't long before a torrent of tears began to flow. I don't know how long I sat there like that, but I couldn't stop crying. All the suffering and misery of the past few years were looking for a way out. There was no stopping it. Eventually I fell asleep that first night with my clothes still on.

NOTE:

Yet, I remain silent. I don't want anyone to know my story. I am terribly ashamed and feel guilty. One has to come up with the right entrance, the right word to wake me up, to soften my mood, a heart to understand me Since I don't come across it so I shut down my sensitivity, block it.

I let my heart grow cold because I no longer have any trust in people around me and don't want to suffer anymore. I was judged for my out-bursts and the cry for help behind them was not listened to. I silence the little girl who complains in me and make her shut up because she is not given the space and the right to scream.

For a long time, I hated that girl inside me and denied and pushed her away for years. There were two personnel inside me. Now I know I have to accept that girl, that girl she never was allowed to be.

On My Own Feet

I WANTED TO get away from my foster-parents. I was not safe there. Now I was finally free but at the same time I didn't know what to do with that freedom.

It's the year 1972 and I had turned sixteen. I had to take care of myself and had no idea how to do that. I had never boiled an egg before, let alone fried it. With the social worker I had bought also a few pans but what to do with pans if you can't cook?

In middle school you don't learn how to cook and my foster-mom never let me in the kitchen when she was cooking. I didn't know the difference between spinach and lettuce and I didn't know how long to boil an egg either. So I had to start creatively and bought all kinds of canned food. All you had to do was heat it up and then you could eat it like that. Easy. There was also no one to ask for advise and also I was to proud for that. I just muddled along my way and it went fine.

My foster-parents had abandoned me. My oldest half-sister was married and lived far away. My other half-sister was married, had her own life and was not interested in me at all. Friends from school I no longer had because they had a carefree schooltime. I had a job and took care of myself now, washing by hand, ironing, shopping etc. I felt very alone and was therefor regularly in the pub. My regular pub was close to the school and often frequented by the children of the school so I maintained some of those contacts anyway. I also visited Dirk-Jan regularly. He supported me wherever he could. I had a hard time, especially in the beginning. With my foster-parents I was kept very short (according to biblical rules) and if you get all that freedom from one day to another, it brings risks, also considering my age of course.

The first month on my own I lived on chips, tinned food and beer. The social worker came by once a month and then I made sure I was at my best of course. When she would ask me how it was all going I always would answer it was going well. She was then always pleased with me. We would talk about my work and some other trivial matters and then she would be gone again. I found it amazing that in all those difficult years in foster care I never saw, let alone spoke to a social worker. Never even asked if everything was going well with me. When the social worker came by, it was always during school hours to talk to my foster-mom. By the time I got home from school the social worker had disappeared. Never, all these years, I did see or speak to one. Now they made time for me, but still my questions were not answered regarding my real parents. They were just not talked about as if they never existed, as if I had not a father and a mother. At the time, I just resigned myself to that for a while because I had other things on my head...survival.

One evening, I was having a beer in my favorite pub again and two boys came in and sat next to me at the bar. We started to have a conversation and one boy of them had my special interest from the moment they came in. His name was Klaas. I had never seen him there before and I told him so. He explained he was living in another city name Heerenveen which was about 30 km. away from Leeuwarden, where I lived. He was a few years older than myself but he was really cute. I liked him and I could tell he like me too. Soon became clear that we fell for each other. A complete new feeling came over me, a feeling I never experienced before. I think I fell in love with this nice boy with his curly blond hair. He invited me to go to his home that evening and because I trusted him I said yes.

He promised me to bring me the next morning back cause I had to go to my job. I was in love for the first time in my life and it was a great, overwhelming feeling. Never before I had felt this way. I stayed overnight and the next morning he drove me back as promised. For the first time I had the feeling I was not alone. I had a boyfriend. I was in love and someone was really interested in me. Soon I was more at his place then in my own little room.

Klaas his parents were divorced and his mother married for second time and lived with two smaller sisters and little brother above the dry-cleaning shop his mother ran. Next to the dry-cleaning shop there was a barber shop and Klaas rented a room above that shop same as his older sister Anna, who also had a room there. The whole family was close to each other and it was a lovely family. Klaas his mom was a real mom, a very warm, lovely woman. I liked her from the beginning and they accepted me all straight into the family, like a warm bath. Such a good feeling they gave me. In no time I called his mother also mom. After a few months of being together we decided to move in together. Driving up and down every day was to much. Every morning and evening all together was 120 km. 5 days a week. In July 1973 we got a flat and I quit my job at the bank. Soon I found a new job at another bank close to our new home (AMRO bank) and started working there as a desk clerk for four days a week. Klaas didn't have a regular job. He was a watchmaker by profession. At home he repaired watches but that was not a secure job, no secure income.

I had not informed the social worker that we were now living together and I never asked her permission. She didn't visited me every month anymore and I was fine with that. I was happy and finely had a life. After we moved to our flat she called me and wanted to make an appointment for a visit. I told her that I was living with my boyfriend and she was surprised. When she came for a chat I told her I changed job also. Because I was only 17 years old she wanted at least to get engaged for form's sake, and we did. In her report she wrote:

Janna had lived with Klaas since July 1973. In October 1973 they got engaged. There were some problems around finding a job. See the financial file for this. She has been on sick leave for a few weeks because of torn ankle ligaments sustained while water-skiing. Since the first of December she has been working at AMRO bank for four days a week. Klaas is still unemployed but will probably get a new job soon. They have a cat and since a few weeks a dog too. Janna had years of flute lessons and played in a wind orchestra. There was a period when she wanted to continue in music.

On the outside, everything looked spotless but the truth was different. We were actually too young to be living together and I had a backpack with me but didn't talk about it. Still I kept it inside, my secret. I was a closed book. Klaas for sure was not ready for living together. No feelings of responsibility what so ever. He got very spoiled by his grandmother who always gave him money, ironed for him, cooked for him etc. I was actually a disturbing factor for her, a danger who maybe would take her grandson away from her. Klaas also started increasingly going out with his friend and that was not doing our relation any good. Slowly our relation became like a traffic light until the day I came home more early then expected and found him in bed with another girl. For me that was the reason to end our relation however painful this was for me because I really loved him very much. He was my first and great love. Luckily I was sweetly taken care of by his family and especially Mom. Still, I felt hurt and terribly let down again.

NOTE:

I felt the need to isolate myself with my grief, blow and forget. I am listless with grief and pain, tired of all I had already been through, jaded by life. I don't exist, I breathe, that's all. But I have to move on and so I do. I go on without knowing why. I go on, aimless and restless. I play roles, but am not myself.

A New Start

I WANTED TO leave Heerenveen. There was nothing left there for me. I felt betrayed.

One day I saw an ad in the newspaper where they were asking for stewardesses on a boat sailing on the river Rhian, from Amsterdam to Basel. This was an excellent opportunity for me to leave Heerenveen behind me because it hurt to see Klaas with his new girlfriend every time. I was ready for a new chapter. I applied for the job and was hired. I wanted to detach from my past and learn to trust people again. I stopped the rent of my flat, packet my things and started this new adventure.

However there was still something I wanted to do before I left. Still I had no answers regarding my past and I had decided to go to the foundation for youth and family (who were responsible for me) to demand the reports written about me. Maybe that way I could find out the truth regarding my origins. By train I went to Groningen, a big city in the north of Holland, where the head office was. Arriving at the office I told them what I wanted: to read all the files related to me. At first, they did not want to accommodate me in that but I was determinated and told them it was my right. I also told them that I would not leave any sooner than I had seen my file. After arguing for a while, I was hands an envelope with some papers. I took the envelope and left the office, On the train back home I opened the envelope and started reading. Nothing in these papers took me much further regarding my parents because nothing was mentioned about them. It just said they had died but I already knew that. What was new for me what they wrote about me and my sisters. It said that we were half-sisters. We had same mother but all three a different father. Also in the envelope were reports in which social workers had written down their findings, following their visits. I was disappointed and felt that my trip had basically been for nothing. I was still as far along in my knowing about my past as I was before the trip. What was the big secret?

25 of March I boarded the boat "Rex Rheni" which means "king of the Rhian river". It was in the water of Leeuwarden that moment and nearby Heerenveen. I had stored my few contents and was ready for a new adventure. Maybe I could leave the bad memories behind? I never had been abroad before and to my mind I was now going out into the wide world. This passenger ship sailed along the river Rhian through Germany to Basel in Switserland. On board it was hard working and we made long hours. We were grossly under paid. However I did have a lot of fun with the other girls on board. We had stops in Amsterdam, Rudesheim, Koblenz, Strassbourg and Basel. It did me good to be away from Heerenveen, from the Netherlands where I left so much pain behind.

I did not stay working on the boat for the whole season. After a few months I disembarked in Amsterdam and stayed there to live. I thought it would be nice to live in a metropolis like Amsterdam but I was actually very disappointed. So many people who were all so preoccupied with themselves. I didn't know anyone there and felt lonely despite all those people around me. I worked for an employment agency at the municipality of Amsterdam in the human resources department. I stayed about six months in Amsterdam and through a friend I had met on the boat, I moved to Schiedam, a small town under the smoke of Rotterdam. She had there a spacious flat and I moved in with her until I found something for myself. Also in Schiedam I worked for an employment agency at the town hall of Rotterdam, city development department until I was offered a permanent job at the music school in Rotterdam. After all my wandering around, I returned to calmer waters but the desire to know my background was still there. Who was I, where were my roots.

I started suffering from severe headaches a lot. Every morning I got up with headaches that tremble all day. I went on sick-leave because I couldn't work with those headaches either. The doctor referred me to a psychologist to talk. I went there three times to talk and then didn't go again. The psychologist was digging into my past so much that it made me very depressed. I wanted to forget, forget about the sexual abuse, the rapes, the humiliations and I had hidden it deep down. He wanted to bring everything to the surface but I was not ready for that. It was my dark secret.

One day I was reading the newspaper and an advertisement caught my eye that appealed to me immensely. A country style band was looking for a singer. You could do an audition the following Saturday and God knows why I decided to go. I never sung in public before, only played the flute. It seemed like a nice opportunity to get back into music. I applied for the audition and was invited. When I arrived that Saturday I saw that there were as many as thirty girls and that moment I wasn't so sure of myself anymore. They were beautiful girls, modernly dressed and much more free-spirited than I had ever been. Ideally, I turned back to go home because who did I think I was. I regretted signing up. Still, I forced myself to stay and heard several girls auditioning. At one point, it was my turn and the song I had chosen to sing was "Stand by your man" from Tammy Wynette. It went better than I expected and at the end, when all girls had sung their songs, we got the results on who would be the new singer of the band. I was very surprised when I was told that I had been chosen. Finely I was back to music, something I had pushed to the background in recent years. My headaches lessened and slowly stayed completely gone

My years in Schiedam

I WAS STILL working at the music school in Rotterdam and I had found a nice little house for myself so I was living alone again. I had little furniture and wanted to redecorate this house to make it my special little place. I decided to look for an aside job for a few evenings per week to make some extra money. I found that quite quickly when I responded to an advert asking for a nanny. I had to look after a baby for an unmarried mother who worked some nights at the red lights in Den Haag. It was for three evenings per week so perfect. It was a baby boy and a sweet little fellow. Most of the time it was sleeping so it was an easy job. After about three months she didn't need me anymore and her boyfriend, Nikos, also the father of the baby, had a suggestion for me for another job. He asked me if I was interested in working in a bar, This bar was located in the south of Rotterdam better known these days as the red light zone. The name of the bar was "The Green Island" and it was actually a brothel. I decided to give it a try to see if I would like it. My job would be bartender. It was a completely different world to me and it was a well-paid job. Three girls worked in front of the bar. Birgitte came from Germany, Liza from Portugal and Roula was from Greece. The owners of the bar, Rizza and Panagioties were also Greek and a really nice couple. I liked the job and made good money. I worked three nights per week. Soon I had saved enough money to buy new furniture. I went painting and wall-papering and I was happy and proud of myself. Still, I kept working in the bar because I had got my driving license and did want to buy a nice car. For the three girls, who worked as prostitutes, I had became a talking point. When they had to go to the doctor I went with them. When they had another problem they always came to me.

Meanwhile, I was 21 years old and one day when I came home from work I found a large, brown envelope on the doormat. The sender was Youth and Family foundation, who had been responsible for me all these years. Now I turned in 21 years old and therefore an adult. Their responsibility for me ended here. There were all kind of papers in the envelope from my parents like old insurance papers that I couldn't do anything with. Not important papers were in there that I could possible use....nothing, not even an accompanying letter. It felt to me like: we are rid of you now and just figure it out yourself. Very cold. Much later, in 2015, I will finely make them pay the price for their disinterested, arrogant behavior. Payback time.

My life went on and I continued to work at the bar a few nights a week. One evening Nikos came over with a Greek friend of his. His name was Manolis and he was a friendly, slightly shy person. Manolis had a charismatic appearance and he somehow captivated me. I asked Rizza for some information about him and she told me he was from Crete and had also a bar together with his brother Vasilis in Rotterdam center name the "Dolphin Bar". She said that he was married to a Dutch woman but it was a bad marriage because his wife was an alcoholic. Manolis and Nikos regularly visited the bar and I got on very well with Manolis. We spoke mostly English with each other because I didn't speak Greek and his Dutch was not that good. One evening Manolis invited me to have a drink with him after finishing my shift and I accepted the invitation. I did want to get to know him better. After closing time he picked me up and we went into town for a drink together, After this first appointment more followed and we became good friends. Manolis treated me with great respect. When he brought me home he never came in. Up to the door and never further because it would be bad for my reputation he said. A woman alone with a man inside would make people talk about me and would give me a bad name. He became a very good friend and always treated me correctly. Life was good to me. I had my job at the music school, three evenings at the bar, the band where I could sing and make my music, yes, life was good. How could I know it was about to change soon again.

One evening, I didn't have to work in the bar and was at home when Rizza called me and I could hear panic in het voice. She was talking fast and confusingly and said something terrible had occurred that evening. I understood from her story that there had been a shooting and that Manolis and Nikos were at the police station. I decided to go to Rizza's house to hear the whole story in a clear way because I didn't understand it all very well. When I arrived in her house I tried to calm her down so she could tell her story clearly so I could understand what had happened that evening.

The Dolphin bar had been closed for a few weeks for a major renovation and was due to reopen that week. The interior had been completely revamped. This particular evening around fifteen Greeks came in. They worked on a ship which was in the harbor of Rotterdam and they were having a good night out. The bar was still closed but the door was open. They were all drunk and started trashing the newly remodeled bar. A struggle ensued and they were ejected from the bar. About one hour later, Manolis and Nikos left the bar. They were driving towards the house of Nikos and on the way they had to wait in front of a red traffic light exactly opposite a nightclub named "the Acropolis". Just as they were standing there waiting in the car, some Greeks came walking out from the Acropolis. These were Greeks who vandalized Manolis his bar a few hours earlier. They saw Manolis and Nikos sitting in the car and started working Manolis his BMW with broken glasses. Manolis and Nikos of course couldn't tolerate this and they got out of the car, ready for another fight. The group Greeks ran back inside the Acropolis and Manolis and Nikos went after them into the bar. It was very crowded inside and what really happened remains a mystery. One shot…Consternation…. A dead person. Police came and the boat crew pointed out Manolis and Nikos. Manolis in particular was singled out as the main perpetrator. However, the weapon was never found.

This was serious and I realized it would be a long time before I would see Manolis again. There was an investigation, a trial and Manolis was sentenced to four years in prison. He was transferred to a prison in Veenhuizen not close to Rotterdam. Later I would learn that my step-father also had been in this prison where he had taken his own life. Visiting rights I did not have, only family and of course his wife. Through his brother Vasilis we maintained contact and wrote letters to each other. Vasilis also arranged that I could visit every now and then when Manolis his wife didn't feel like going. Often I went in her place. I barely spoke a word of Greek and started a course Greek conversation. Our letter exchange also helped me study Greek language. Since Schiedam was quite far from Veenhuizen, I decided to move closer to prison. The visiting hours were every Monday from 1pm to 4pm. His wife pretty soon stopped coming at all so I went every Monday. I found a holiday home in a small village named Appelscha and was sure I would find another job again. My period in Rotterdam was over and a new period dawned for me.

Back to the North

THE HOLIDAY COTTAGE was in the middle of the forests of Appelscha and I loved it immediately. In Schiedam, I lived in the hustle and bustle and here I was in the middle of nature with only the sound of birds and otherwise peace and quiet.

Since I needed an income anyway, I kept working in the bar in Rotterdam three days a week for the first few months. Two nights I was able to stay in a flat above the bar and on the third night I drove back to

Appelscha after work. Manolis didn't like that at all and sent his brother to me to give me money so I wouldn't have to work but I refused to take that money. wanted to support myself and never have to say 'thank you' again, something I had promised myself the day my foster parents had dumped me. I never wanted to depend on anyone again. Every Monday afternoon, I visited Manolis from 1pm to 4pm. I supported him because he was having a tough time in there. We philosophized a lot and he told me about his childhood in Crete. I had never been there before but how he talked about it sounded great.

Appelscha was in fact a small village and because of my arrival there, there was speculation pretty soon. I came from the big city to live in such a small village, for what reason, what was my business there? According to the gossip, I had worked probably as a prostitute and was now on the run from something or someone. Funny how people can make up their own truth. I did not go on the defensive and thought it was all fine. After a few months, I found a new job in a town close by and luckily I no longer had to drive up and down to Rotterdam.

I did still visit Rotterdam regularly because we were recording with the band in the studio for our first album. It became my first album. When my album 'Blond Illusion' was released, people in the village started looking at me differently and also became a bit friendlier.

At that time, I decided to travel to Nieuweschans, my home village, with a good friend of mine to look for my parents' graves. I still did not know then that my stepfather was not my real father. We found my stepfather's grave but could not find my mother's. After a few hours of searching, we went into a cafe for a cup of coffee. There was an old man behind the bar and two men in their forties sat at the bar. At one point, I asked the little old man behind the bar if he knew my father and mentioned his name, Jan Kerkhof. A silence fell and before the little boss could answer me, the one man at the bar said to the other:' That's the guy who hanged himself in his cell'. Again a silence fell and apparently I turned very pale because the old boss called his wife and she took me to the living area. She gave me another cup of coffee so I could recover a bit from the shock. In a very cruel way, I had become a bit wiser.

Unfortunately I had to leave the holiday cottage because its owner approached me in a sexual manner every time he visited. He and his wife ran a snack bar in the village. I was not happy with his attempts and groping and threatened to tell his wife. He kicked me out. Soon I found another shelter. There was a sweet little farmhouse empty in the middle of the meadow and someone from the village gave me the owner's phone number. I called and asked if I could rent it. The owner agreed almost immediately and we made an appointment to discuss everything and to hand me the key. The little farmhouse was so cute and I was very happy with it. The rent was very reasonable and I felt I was very lucky. One evening, I was in the village café having a glass of wine and some boys from the village were also sitting at the bar. One of them was Ruud. Ruud was a quiet boy and worked for himself so he told me. He worked in the forest with his tractor and horse. Together with the other boys, he cut down trees, dragged the tree trunks out of the forest with the horse, and with the tractor, the tree trunks were laid by the side of the road to be sawn into meter pieces. The boys earned 100 guilders a day which was a very good salary. I asked Ruud if I could join them for a day too. They all laughed because, they said, this was not a job for girls. I made a deal with Ruud that I would go with him the next day and that he would only have to pay me if it turned out at the end of the day that I had done my job well. Well, they all wanted to experience that and so, no sooner said than done. The next morning, I was picked up at 7pm to go to work. The boys saw it as a big joke but I was very serious. Coincidentally, they were working in the forest where the prison was also, Veenhuizen. My job was to use the tractor's grapple to pick up the logs to drag them to the road, where they were cut into meter pieces. Sawing was also my job. Heavy work, that was for sure but I worked hard and was able to keep up with everyone. The boys weren't so loud anymore and were impressed. By the end of the working day, I had proved myself and got paid. The guys had respect for me. When I got home, however, I was exhausted and without food I went straight into my bed. went along for a few weeks except, of course, on Mondays because then it was visiting time. Manolis had already heard the news from guards about my work in the forest and was absolutely not happy about it and even angry. I didn't care because I wanted to earn money. Nothing wrong with that. We had also had a nice trade with the inmates who were in the open facility. They were allowed to roam freely during the day. Most of them were alcoholics. For the horse, there was a horse trailer in the forest where the horse went at night. During the day, these inmates would put their order for alcohol in the trailer, under the straw and we would carry out that order and put it in the trailer the next morning. Everyone happy. One day, disaster struck. I was busy working on the tractor. It was winter and in the afternoon the sun was low in the sky. The moment I drove out of the forest with the tractor and with the peg full of tree trunks, a VW van came from the right containing two prison guards. They were driving on the left side of the road at high speed while having little visibility due to the low sun. Because they were driving on the wrong side of the road, they hit the front of the tractor I was riding on. This gave a huge bang and the tractor broke in two. The front part of the tractor flew over a ditch into the forest and I was still on the rear part. The VW van ended up 50 meters away. What I remember is that I heard the diesel flowing and like a robot I climbed off the tractor, walked to the van in shock and sat down in the grass next to the van. I stared at the driver who was stuck groaning in pain and could not get out. I was in a state of shock. Soon the sirens of the prison complex were blaring and first aid arrived. The co-driver was not that seriously injured but for the driver it did not look good. It would later be revealed that his liver was ruptured and he had several other injuries. The impact was also very big. After this accident, I didn't want to go on the tractor. I knew the accident was not my fault but I felt terrible that it had happened.

During Manolis' detention, he received word from Crete that his mother was in hospital and they didn't give her long time anymore. He applied for a week's leave to go to Crete to see his mother once more. However, this leave was rejected and there was no time for a second application. So he asked me to go to Crete in his place and visit his mother in hospital. Of course I wanted to do this for him. I left on May 2, 1981 (I was 24 years old) for Athens, where his older brother lived with his wife and two children. In Athens, I would stay for a week before flying to Crete to Chania. The brother worked in the navy and was very nice. I had a wonderful week in Athens. After that week, I went to Crete and was picked up by half of the family from the airport. When we were almost at his father's house, I heard loud gunshots. His father was shooting into the air, which meant "welcome." This was my first encounter with Crete but it would leave a mark on the rest of my life. How hopelessly I fell in love with this island, the people, the culture, the language, and the music. Crete became a part of me at that moment because it felt like coming home. The family was good to me and together with Manolis's father, I visited the hospital where his mother was ill. What a lovely woman. I saw the sadness in her eyes because she wouldn't be able to see her son anymore. I saw and felt her sadness for her son who was in prison in a distant land and from whom she could not say goodbye. Her son whom she could no longer hold in her arms. It took another month after my departure back to the Netherlands before she died. I supported Manolis where I could.

A New Challenge

As I mentioned earlier, I was working on the recordings of my debut album "Blond Illusion". It featured country-rock classics like "It's so easy to fall in love and "It's a heartache". I was very proud of this project and a dream came true for me. I was busy, busy because I was studying again and taking courses to finally obtain my unfinished high school diploma. I also got my diploma in beauty therapy and my hospitality diploma. When the country album was released, I had many performances. I released the album independently and sold it during the performances. Everything went as planned. Manolis, on the other hand, was less enthusiastic about everything I undertook and didn't like that I was traveling all over the country for performances. He had served most of his sentence and was allowed to have leave every weekend. Naturally, he would then go to his business in Rotterdam and expected me to go with him. He was already divorced from his wife and I think the idea was that I would take her place. However, I had other plans. I wanted to be free and make my own dreams come true. Manolis did not understand that my album and performances were important to me, and he was very disappointed in me. We grew apart, and when he was finally released, he naturally went back to Rotterdam. I did not follow and stayed in Appelscha. We let each other go. Later I heard that he remarried a woman from Yugoslavia. I hope he has found his happiness.

I wasn't really looking for love, but during a performance, I came across a new love that would turn my life upside down again. His name was Victor and he came from Portugal and worked in a pizzeria. I fell in love very much. He was handsome and funny, a nice guy. However, he was illegal in the Netherlands because Portugal was not yet in the EEG at that time. He needed a work and residence permit to be able to work and live in the Netherlands, but he did not have one. The owner of the pizzeria where he worked was an Italian friend of his. Soon, Victor was at my place more than in his own apartment, and also quite quickly he stopped working at the pizzeria. I wasn't too happy about it because now he had no income. Actually, this was the first red flag that I pushed under the table. Stupid of me but I was in love and blinded. It was 1983 when I met Victor, and initially things went quite well. We had a lot of fun together and usually he would come along when I had a performance. We had to be frugal because he had no income and I had an irregular income. However, more red flags passed by, especially regarding his behavior after consuming alcohol. I also pushed those signals under the table because I wanted so badly to stay on my pink cloud. I wish I hadn't done that because I have had to pay dearly for it. Because Appelscha was a small community, the village soon knew that I was living with Victor, and it was only a matter of time before he was betrayed. He received a letter stating that he had to leave the Netherlands within a month. That was quite a shock because what were we to do? What was I to do? Should I let him go and leave him to depart alone? We had already been on vacation in Portugal once and I thought it was a beautiful country with friendly people. I was faced with a difficult decision and didn't have much time to think about this problem. Victor really wanted me to go with him. He said that we could first go to Belgium to work there to earn some money and then go from Belgium to Portugal. In the end, I agreed and we started packing. I had to store my belongings again and informed the owner of the small farm. I sold my car and we left for Belgium by train, heading to Brussels. I was starting a new adventure.

It would be the dumbest decision I have ever made in my life, but I didn't know that at the time.

Brussels...Belgium

CHAPTER 12

WHEN WE ARRIVED in Brussels, we slept in a hotel for the first night. The next day we had to look for a room. We looked in the newspapers for rooms for rent and visited several to see if it was something. In the end, we took a room in Saint Josse ten Node near the European Parliament building. We settled in Rue Marie Therese number 49 where we had found a not too spacious attic room. The room was furnished but not with much luxury. A big difference from my snugly little farmhouse. Anyway, this was it and I had to settle for it. In the end, it would only be for a few months and then we would leave for Portugal. We didn't have much with us either so we didn't need much space. The first thing I was going to do after we moved into the room was to search the newspapers for a job. I noticed that staff in Brussels all had to be bilingual. Flemish and French. I soon found a job in a coffee bar in the center of Brussels and within a week I was back at work. With Victor, things didn't go so fast, unfortunately, and this caused the first annoyances, especially on my part. I thought I had worked long enough for two and wanted him to do something too. Through my work in the coffee bar, I also got in touch pretty quickly with people who were interested in my singing career. I was invited for appearance, interviews for newspapers and an interview for a radio station. Thus began the annoyances for Victor. He couldn't quite stomach the fact that I was fully engaged and he felt he was just hanging around. He felt he was dwarfed by me and that was bad for his ego. Slowly Victor changed and there was often a lot of tension between us. Eventually, he did find a job in a restaurant where he could work every night. We didn't see much of each other anymore because I worked mostly during the day. I worked long hours and ate poorly because Victor ate at the restaurant where he worked and regularly I was sick. On my 27th birthday (Dec 1983), I was in bed with a middle ear infection.

Victor was very nervous and took it all out on me. The first terrible incident occurred in the first days of January 1984. At the pet shop, I had seen a small kitten sitting in the window as I drove past it on the tram. I instantly fell in love and because I missed animals around me I wanted to take that kitten home. I often felt sad and lonely. Victor agreed to the kitten and so I took the kitten into our home. One afternoon, Victor came home and I was on the bed over the covers playing with the little kitten. I noticed that Victor had been drinking so I was wary. He was irritated about something but I didn't know the reason. I decided to ignore him and say nothing and continued to play with the kitten. Suddenly, Victor grabbed the creature from me and smacked it full force against the wall. The creature slid down the wall and remained motionless on the floor. I was in shock and completely upset and crying I picked up the little animal and later buried it. I did not speak because intuitively I knew this would not be healthy for me. I turned inside myself and suffered in silence. Victor went to sleep.

He changed more and more and I didn't recognize him anymore. Things were not going the way he wanted and he had a certain jealousy towards me that made him nervous and combined with alcohol, an uncontrolled aggression took possession of him. He became a walking powder keg and I realized that very well. I was walking on eggshells. It scared me because he became unpredictable. I knew I was in danger but didn't quite know what to do with it. On the night of January eight to nine, things went badly wrong, I had been upset for a week because of the event with the cat and it was difficult for me to be friendly with Victor anymore. I was too angry, too much still in shock and couldn't just get over it. Victor sensed this but he didn't even apologize either.

The evening of January eight I was home because I had worked all day and I was tired. Victor went to work at the restaurant. I decided to go to bed nice and early. Around half past three that night, I heard Victor coming home. He was making a lot of noise and I understood that he had been drinking quite a bit. He had probably still gone out after work and drank whisky. I woke up and knew immediately how things stood. I saw it in his eyes. At that moment, it wouldn't have mattered what I would or wouldn't have said because he was out for a fight and then he didn't need a reason. Suddenly he came and sat on top of me while I was under the covers. With his left hand he restrained my hands in an iron grip above my head and with his right fist he started pounding on my face, one after the other I got the full load. He hit my eyes, my nose, my mouth, my cheeks and everywhere he could hit me. The first blows hurt a lot but at some point I no longer felt the blows. I turned my head to one side and that was all I could do. I felt my warm blood running down my face and I could only wait for him to finish.... His eyes turned in his head and the only thing that went through me was that these would be the last moments of my life. He continued to pound on me until I sank unconscious into a black pit. He probably felt me going limp and came back to his senses and stopped. When I regained consciousness, he was still on me and crying like a small child. He realized what he had done during his rage attack. The bed was completely red with blood. The wall behind the bed was full of blood splattered up to the ceiling. I could hardly see anything because my eyes were closed and filled with blood. I could also barely speak and I waited, I waited for things to come. What else could I do?

Finally Victor stepped away from me and walked around the room pondering how to solve this. I too was thinking how to escape from this situation. I begged him to call an ambulance because I knew I was seriously injured and needed to go to hospital. Victor was not comfortable with that of course because questions would be asked.

Helplessly, I lay in bed in my own blood, unable to do anything for myself. I was at his mercy but he did not know how to handle the situation. I kept begging him to take me to the hospital but he was clearly panicking. It took till 9pm before he made a decision. I had to promise that I would not tell anyone he had done this. He made up another story which I had to tell if the police asked about it. I had to tell that I had been attacked by purse-snatching thieves in the streets. At that point, I had promised anything if only I could get out of that room. My head was so swollen to as much as two times its normal size and could barely see anything, only in a blur. I was at his mercy and his good will and so yes, I promised anything he wanted to hear. Finally, he called a taxi and helped me stumble down the stairs, into the taxi. The driver said nothing at all and dropped us off at the hospital. At reception, I was immediately put on a stretcher and Victor had to fill in the necessary paperwork. He put everything in my name as we were not insured. I was examined by doctors, cleaned and put on an infusion. My lips were stitched as they were torn. Through the drip, I was given painkillers and a sleeping drug as I was totally upset. Only at the hospital could I let my emotions out because there had been no room for that before. It was as if I had ended up in the wrong film. The doctors were all super nice to me and although I had initially felt joy on arrival (relief), when I lay in that hospital bed it turned into sadness and a terrible feeling of loneliness. For the umpteenth time in my life, I was so alone again and had no one to fall back on. I was in a strange land with only strangers around me. Victor I did not see again that day, the coward. The police came in the afternoon when I was awake. I dared not tell the truth and so I told Victor's version about four boys who had robbed me in the street.

Ten days I spent in hospital. My face swollen and a pinching nerve on the right side that caused a lot of pain and a paralytic sensation. To this day, that feeling has not returned either. Victor visited the hospital on the third day and was shocked by what he had done. My face was blue/purple/red, all the colors of the rainbow. He behaved exemplary and said he was very sorry. He proudly told me that he had had the bedding washed, the blankets steamed and would still replace the wallpaper on the wall. When I was discharged from the hospital, I ended up in a clean bed. ow, I was so lucky. I let everything he said wash over me. I was numb, my feelings were numb, as if I were in some kind of shock. Nothing interested me anymore, nothing was important to me anymore. I felt humiliated, betrayed, and above all, I was angry with myself for letting it get this far and I blamed myself for everything. When Victor left after visiting hours, an Italian doctor came to my bedside and asked how I was doing. He watched Victor walk out of the room and said to me, 'He did this to you, didn't he?' Something inside me broke and all my emotions came flooding out, and I nodded in agreement. Finally, someone knew this terrible secret, and I could share the burden with this doctor. He gave me something to calm me down, and I fell into a deep sleep. I was completely exhausted and just wanted to sleep.

NOTE:

My pain overwhelms everything and I can no longer suppress it. I am overflowing and no longer want to make an effort to smile; I no longer feel like putting on a façade, being in control of things. I don't want to make an effort to keep going anymore. I don't want to look ahead any-more. It's exhausting me. The outside world frightens me, I do not belong there and feel so vulnerable. Everything feels like a threat.

After ten days, I was discharged from the hospital and Victor came to pick me up and took me back to the room where the nightmare had taken place. There were flowers in a vase, coffee and cake were served, and Victor was in a very good mood. It was clear that he wanted to put this incident behind him as quickly as possible so that he could get on with his life.

To Portugal

AFTER MY FACE had turned every color of the rainbow, it slowly began to improve. I had to return to the hospital several times because a nerve was pinched and causing severe pain. My teeth and jaw also needed some work because everything was damaged. A great deal of tension had arisen between Victor and me because I no longer trusted him. He, on the other hand, was as sweet as pie. I couldn't be intimate with him anymore, I just couldn't bring myself to do it. After a few weeks at home, I finally went back to work. I had run out of money and needed to work again to save up. I demanded that Victor find another job and not work in the hospitality industry anymore. He really tried hard to find another job and found one in a garage. He started painting cars.

I wanted to leave Brussels, and Victor promised that life in Portugal would be better for us. I decided to give him another chance, although I was very cautious and walked on eggshells. We bought a car, an Opel Record 2100 D station wagon, and in June 1984 we drove to Portugal. I felt hopeful again that everything would turn out well because Victor was in a great mood. I wanted so badly to believe that he had learned something from his outburst.

When we arrived in Portugal, we went straight to visit his mother and sister, who lived in Lisbon. We would stay there until we found something of our own. His mother was a small woman who walked with crutches and complained twenty-four hours a day. She was divorced, and Victor's sister lived with her. His sister also spent the whole day talking about how difficult things were for her and her mother and that they needed money. It didn't make me any happier because Victor kept giving them money. After a few weeks, we had already made a significant dent in our savings, and I cautiously began to discuss finding work and a place to live. I wanted to distance myself from his family. I also expected Victor to find work easily now that he was back in his own country, but he wasn't in such a hurry to find a job. He also believed that we were comfortable staying with his family, so why rent something for ourselves? I understood that he would not keep his promises and was disappointed. I was not happy with the situation and understood that I had to take action myself. I took some of my albums with me and visited a few artist agencies. I left an album with my phone number at each one. I didn't have to wait long. The first to call was Mr. Peres from the artist agency 'Interartes'. He asked me to come by for an interview and was very interested in me. When I arrived at his office, he offered me a contract to perform for three weeks at the casino in Funchal on the beautiful island of Madeira from 22 October till 14 November 1984. Of course, I was over the moon because this was beyond my wildest dreams. I would be starring in an international show in Madeira for three weeks and getting paid well for it. Travel and accommodation were also fully reimbursed, and of course I signed the contract. Victor wanted to come along, but he had to pay for his own ticket. It would be a few more weeks before we were due to leave for Madeira, and now that I had this contract in my pocket, it was time to find an apartment. Of course, I found one. We moved to the other side of the Tagus River.

The plane to Madeira departed on 22 October at 9 p.m. In the afternoon, I had a rehearsal with the other artists and the ballet. Due to Victor's actions, we missed the plane and another plane did not depart until the afternoon. I was angry because I was already tense and nervous enough about this big adventure, and now I had missed the rehearsal too. Fortunately, everything turned out fine and that same evening was my debut, and it all went great. I had my own dressing room, worked with international artists and was also well paid. However, Victor was a disruptive factor because his jealousy resurfaced. He told everyone that he was my manager and that he had produced my album. He annoyed me to death because he only told lies. He wanted to be important at my expense. When I was on stage, he was sitting in the audience in a suit with a whisky in his hands, and I felt that fear again because I didn't know how the whisky would go down. All that stress had caused me to lose a lot of weight, and I often felt nauseous.

After three weeks of performances at Zodiac Casino Funchal, I had to say goodbye to my dear fellow artists, which made me sad because we had become a close-knit team during those weeks. We flew back to Lisbon and the tensions between Victor and me grew again. He still didn't have a job and wasn't looking for one either. I was working for him and his family, and I didn't agree with that at all. I knew I didn't want to continue with this relationship. I was afraid of him and no longer had feelings for him. All his negative traits came back. He was authoritarian, jealous and arrogant, especially now that he was back in his own country. After the assault in Brussels, he didn't touch me again, but in Portugal, when he went out with friends, I made sure I didn't stay at home that night. I didn't go home until the next day. I knew this would be better for me.

In December of that year, I was offered another ten-day contract to perform at the casino in Figueira da Foz in northern Portugal, near the city of Porto. I did not allow Victor to accompany me because the money would only be spent on his ticket and his whisky. I remained firm in my decision, and he seemed to accept it. My birthday also fell within those ten days, and of course, he suddenly appeared in front of me. My birthday could have been so much fun, but Victor managed to ruin it for me again. His jealousy took over and he even got into an argument with the casino manager. I was mortified by his behavior. Later, back at my hotel, he argued with me because he was angry that the director opened a bottle of champagne for me on stage, which I drank with the ballet girls. Victor wasn't involved in that, and he was angry about it. That night, I locked myself in the bathroom, and the next day I demanded that he leave, and fortunately, he did.

I tried to save as much money as possible so that I could buy a ticket to escape from this situation. If I told him, he would kill me, I knew that for sure, so I said nothing and had to do everything in secret.

On the 31th December, I had a performance in southern Portugal at Europe's largest golf hotel, the Penina Hotel in Portimao. This is where the wealthiest people from all over Europe and beyond gathered, including the owner of Blizzard skis. I performed at 11:30 a.m. that evening, and fortunately, Victor was not present.

The whole situation was actually very sad. On stage, I was intensely happy, but outside of it, I was deeply unhappy. My intention on that New Year's Eve in 1985 was to escape from this situation and find myself again. With a glass of champagne, I toasted to that thought that evening.

On January 2, 1985, I returned to Lisbon and Victor was not in a good mood because the car was broken. I didn't feel like spending money on it because I knew I wouldn't be able to take the car with me anyway. Victor remained angry and I was depressed and increasingly nauseous. One evening he asked me what was wrong, and I said that I was unbelievably unhappy and wanted to go to the Netherlands for a few weeks. He got furious and said: "Then go to the Netherlands, no money for car repairs but money to go to the Netherlands." So mean to say that because he hadn't worked or earned any money yet, and everyone was living off my money and I told him that too. I was so done with it. When I said this to him, he grabbed me by the neck. I was sitting on a stool and as he squeezed my throat, I fell backward onto the hard floor. He screamed and ranted and kicked me all over my body, in my stomach, everywhere he could touch me. Again I feared for my life. When he was done with me, he threw a cigarette in my face and walked out the door, leaving me on the ground. I realized that I needed to find a way to get away quickly. The sooner the better. I couldn't take it anymore.

At the end of January, I started working as a model at a fashion company in Lisbon. The carnival season began, and there was no room for my repertoire to perform. At the end of February, Victor received a message from his Italian friend for whom he had worked at the pizzeria in the Netherlands. This friend had come to Portugal and wanted to open a pizzeria in the town of Leiria. He asked Victor to come work for him again, and Victor was open to that and so he left for Leiria and I was relieved. By then, I had a new little friend. His name was Gipsy. I had saved this dog from drowning. We were inseparable. After Victor had worked in the restaurant for two weeks, he wanted me to come to Leiria as well. I felt nauseous every day and had a lot of pain in my stomach. I went to Leiria but actually just lay in bed there. I felt sick. Victor called me a lazy pig because he wanted me to work in the restaurant too. I was really not able to do that and didn't want to at all. I only got food if I came to the restaurant, but I was not able to do that anymore either. Sometimes he would bring food after he was done working, but mostly he didn't. I was getting worse and worse, and I wanted to see a doctor. Victor thought I was overreacting but went with me to the doctor to prove that I was fine. The opposite was true because that same evening I was on the operating table in the hospital and my appendix was removed. I was lying on the third floor of the hospital in Leiria and the cockroaches were running across the floor. Dried mold from the walls got into my bed and I had to sweep it out every morning. There was also no nursing staff because in those countries it is customary for your family to take care of you. You do need to have family.

After ten days, I was allowed to go home again, and it was now March. The nausea returned and the stomach pains too. Back at the doctor who concluded after examination that my liver wasn't doing too well either. For me, this was the moment I would take advantage of. For

Victor, I was a burden and useless. When I told him that the healthcare in the Netherlands was actually a bit better and that I preferred to go to the Netherlands for treatment, he agreed with me. I was only allowed to bring Gipsy with me from him, but no other belongings like my beloved flute. The agreement was that I would stay in the Netherlands for two weeks and then return. Whatever, I promised it of course, if I just could leave. I took the bus from Inter-lines and Victor warned me that if I didn't come back he would find me. Whatever!!! as long as I could just leave.

Back to Holland

IN JUNE IT finally happened. Victor took me to the Inter-lines bus and I only had 1 bag with me and Gipsy. Victor really believed that I would come back because I had to leave all my possessions behind, the most important of which was my flute. We said goodbye and I quickly got on the bus and looked for a seat by the window. The bus started to drive and I began to cry. Not from sorrow but from relief. I had finally escaped and was driving towards my freedom. The journey lasted three days and two nights and I really needed that because I had to leave the past two years behind me. The landscape rushed past me and my thoughts were with the past, what wrong choices I had made so far. I tried so hard but managed nothing. I had completely lost myself and still didn't know who I was. I had nothing left and had to start over again. Fortunately, I had my dear Gipsy with me, and together we would make the best of it. The journey went well, and as we got closer to the Netherlands, I became increasingly happier. In recent years, I had occasionally been in contact with my foster parents and from Portugal I called them to ask if I could stay with them for a few days. I couldn't ask anyone else. It wasn't ideal of course, but I didn't have much choice. Maybe they said yes out of guilt, I don't know. I had to put my pride aside in this case and hoped to find something for myself as soon as possible. I stayed with my foster parents for a week, and of course, it did not go well at all. I went to the hospital for examination, and it turned out that I was walking around with a severe stomach ulcer. No appendix, no bad liver. The stomach ulcer was caused by all the stresses.

A week with my foster parents was long enough, so I went to visit Manolis in Rotterdam for a week. After that, I spent ten days with Aunt Truus, a retired midwife whom I had met in Portugal and who also welcomed me with open arms. In the meantime, I had also received word that there was a place for me in Leeuwarden, where I had registered. It wasn't a very big flat, but it was big enough for Gipsy and me. I was happy to finally have my own place again and to be able to settle down. I furnished the flat with my stored belongings and some second-hand furniture, such as a bed. I didn't have a car, so my foster father offered to deliver the bed. Together, we assembled the bed and placed the mattress on top. He pulled me onto the bed, and it became apparent that he had not changed at all. However, he made a significant error in judgement. I had become stronger and taller, and I was no longer willing to be pushed around. I was no longer that little girl he could abuse whenever he felt like it. I pulled myself free and walked out of the bedroom without saying a word. In the future, I would make sure not to be alone in a room with this man again.

Thanks to the medication and rest, my health slowly improved. I gradually gained a few pounds and my life started to get back on track. I started giving private music lessons at home or on location. I bought a second-hand car and slowly climbed out of the valley I had fallen into. I built up a circle of friends again and life was good.

In recent years, I hadn't had time to dwell on my past, but now that I had settled down and was alone again, the desire to know my past and origins returned with a vengeance. As I mentioned earlier, my relationship with my two half-sisters was not close. In the past, they had sought contact with my mother's sisters, who did not want to take us in after my mother's tragic death but instead placed us in an orphanage. One of them called me one day to say that she had visited one of my aunts and that this aunt also had baby photos of me and asked if I wanted them. Yes, I was interested because I didn't have any baby photos of myself. I told her I wanted them. My sister then said that I could pick them up from my aunt. This really rubbed me the wrong way. When I was a baby, she didn't want to know me, and now she actually thought I would come to her for those photos? Nice try and I couldn't believe it. She could stick those photos wherever she wanted.

A Positive Change

MY LIFE IN Leeuwarden was going smoothly, and I had settled into a calmer routine, which I really needed. I was teaching music and Greek conversation classes.

One of my Greek students was Femmie. She came from a village not far from Leeuwarden and travelled back and forth by train every day. Because my apartment was far from the station, I gave her lessons in a hotel opposite the station after she finished work. After class, we always went to a bar next door for a glass of wine, and then she took the train home. That was also the case on that warm day in September. We sat down at the bar and ordered a glass of wine. There were also two men at the bar who had clearly had enough to drink because they were in a boisterous mood. They started talking to us and making jokes. At one point, the smaller of the two said he would like to go out with me sometime. To get rid of him, I agreed, and he gave me his phone number, promising I would call. A few days later, I found the phone number in my bag and decided it would be polite to call and say that I would not be accepting the invitation. He told me that he was co-owner of a café-restaurant in the center of Leeuwarden and expected me to drop by for a glass of wine that Saturday afternoon. That Saturday was beautifully sunny, so I got on my bike to go and drink that glass of wine. I sat down on the terrace and he was working there. He introduced himself as Jan and brought me a dry white wine. He didn't have much time to talk to me because it was very busy. When I was about to leave, he suggested I come by on Tuesday at 7 pm because he would be off work then and we could have dinner together. In the end, I ended up with a date. I liked him and thought dinner wouldn't hurt.

That Tuesday evening, I rode my bike to his café. I deliberately chose to ride my bike so that he could drop me off at my bike after dinner. It was safe and hassle-free, which was exactly what I wanted. I was completely done with men and had lost all trust in them. We went to a pizzeria and had a very pleasant time with lots to talk about. As the evening progressed, I found him increasingly pleasant and interesting. The food was delicious, as was the Chianti wine. It turned out to be a perfect evening. Jan paid the bill and we walked back to his car. He drove back to where my bike was parked, got out, picked up my bike and threw it in the boot of his car. Then he got back in his car and drove away. Full of surprise, I sat next to him in the car, waiting to see what would happen next. Actually, I found his approach quite amusing. We stopped in a small street and Jan got out, took my bike and parked it in front of a house... his house. I got out too and followed him inside. Once we were inside, he put on some classical music, 'The Young Mozart', and excused himself for five minutes. I was sitting on the floor looking at his music collection when he came back into the living room with a large bowl of fruit. All kinds of fruit were on the bowl, cut into pieces and beautifully arranged.

I was very impressed and charmed because he had prepared all this earlier that day. No man had ever done this for me before. He had put a lot of effort into it and did his best to make me comfortable. I felt very comfortable with him, safe, valued, and respected. I decided to trust him.

I beg you, be kind to my feelings,
it will take time because I'm hurt.
I beg you, please be considerate with your words.
It will take time because I have heard too many lies.

I beg you, be kind with your eyes
it will take time because I have seen too much contempt
I beg you, be kind with your body
it will take time because I have felt too many cold bodies.
I beg you, be kind with your love.
There is a beauty in that kindness
that only true love
can understand.

That evening I stayed and in fact I haven't left since. Of course, Gipsy came along to his house too. I actually only came to my apartment to water the plants and pick up the mail. I wasn't planning to give up my apartment because I had learned that lesson. Keep my own place where I could withdraw to, where I could be alone.

The Big Step

I HAD A great time with Jan. He wasn't possessive, not jealous, and respected my independence. He had his job in his whorehouse and I had my job. On Christmas 1987, we went out to dinner at the home of Jan's friends who owned a Yugoslav restaurant. After dinner, we sat comfortably by the fireplace in the restaurant with a glass of cognac. Out of nowhere, Jan asked me to marry him. I definitely did not see this coming because we had only known each other for three months and I had never planned to get married. I didn't really believe in that. I didn't know what to say for a moment, but I got help from a couple who were also sitting by the fireplace. They had heard Jan's proposal, and when I didn't respond, the lady turned to me and said: 'Just say yes,' and I followed her advice and said yes. It all happened very quickly, but it felt good. For Jan, this was his second marriage. It felt like I had known Jan for years, very familiar. In January 1988, we registered for our marriage and the wedding date was set for February third. I had a lot to arrange in that short time and to think about my wedding attire. Somehow I still wanted to win the love of my foster parents (Stockholm syndrome) and thought that they would be proud of me for finally settling down and becoming a 'decent' woman. I called them for an appointment to introduce Jan to them. We went there one morning for a coffee and we had just sat down when the doorbell rang. Through a side window, I saw who was at the door. The pastor was also invited. I got so angry because once again my foster father wanted to take control. My stepfather had invited him to talk with us. I put him in the position to choose: either the pastor would leave or Jan and I would leave. The pastor left. Jan and I were old and wise enough to plan our wedding ourselves and we certainly didn't want to get married in church. My stepfather was not happy with me at all because he had lost his game.

We went together to choose wedding outfits. I didn't want to get married in a dress but in a tuxedo. In a men's shop, I had a tuxedo fitted and I also looked for a nice large black hat. Jan bought a nice gray striped suit and he would wear a fedora with it. We looked good. We had cards printed for the invitations, arranged live music, and chose a restaurant where the party would take place. I didn't know that many people but Jan knew all the more. It turned into a big party. All my students came and I played a duet on the transverse flute with my youngest music student. My half-sisters came too, and I was happy about that. Of course, my stepfather had to pull another stunt. His power game knew no bounds. He came to me and said that he had forgotten the envelope with its contents (gift) but that he would drop it through the mailbox the next morning. Ah, I could expect anything from that man and I pretended that I didn't care. Again he had to humiliate me, he couldn't help himself, but I wasn't planning to let him ruin my party. Dirk-Jan also came and was happy for me. It was good and it was a beautiful day. The envelope with contents was indeed in the hallway the next morning. The contents were 25 guilders. In a painful way, he made me feel again how he thought of me. From now on, I was no longer Jeannette (Janna) Kerkhof but Jeannette Meijer and a new life lay ahead of me. I was 32 years old and married. Who would have ever thought that? I was now a married woman and had to get used to that. It had all happened so quickly. Not only did I have to get used to the name change, but more so to the fact that for the first time in my life I was connected to someone. An English researcher had conducted research into the psychological state of children who had not experienced maternal love in their early years. These children were at high risk of developing irreparable character damage later in life. This researcher introduced the term "attachment". The core of his theory was that if the mother failed to establish a special bond with her child, this would later lead to serious psychological and physical disorders. Even in an orphanage, a child will always have to settle for a surrogate, and the caregiver can never match the love of a parent and the natural bond. I had never felt or experienced true connection with anyone before, and it frightened me a little. Suddenly having a strong bond with someone can be very frightening if you have never known it before. I had never had that bond with my half-sisters, and certainly not with my foster parents. I had told Jan about my past, and it seemed as if he loved me even more because of it. Jan didn't have a particularly pleasant past either and was raised by his grandfather. He had lost contact with his parents and, in fact, with his brothers and sisters as well. His parents were both alcoholics.

One day, Jan decided he wanted to leave the café-restaurant he co-owned. He sold his share and started a handyman business. He was very skilled. He had a lot of work and things were going well. I continued teaching and did the bookkeeping for his new business. At one point, he was offered a big job: renovating a bar in the city center. It was the smallest bar in town, and Jan worked on it for a few months. When it was almost finished, he came home one day and said that the bar was for rent. He thought it might be something for me. I had the necessary experience and the right qualifications. I didn't have to think about it for long and wanted to embark on this new adventure. I signed the five-year lease contract. I wanted to turn it into a kind of music café. I had already thought of a name. The café would be called 'De Blauwe Druif' (The Blue Grape). There was an old piano and a guitar hanging on the wall, and anyone who wanted to could play music. There were peanuts on the bar, and you could throw the shells on the wooden floor. It always had a great atmosphere because it was a small café. Above the bar, I had two more floors, one of which I rented out and the other I kept for myself. The opening was in May 1988.

I also still had my own flat and felt it was time to give it up. We got married in February, but I still had my flat just in case. Jan never said anything about it and didn't push me. He always came along to water the plants, but never said I should give it up. He understood, and that was so sweet. A busy period began because, in addition to my work in the café, I also continued to teach. I worked long hours because I did everything myself... behind the bar, cleaning, taking orders, bookkeeping, etc. When Jan had time, he helped out behind the bar. I organized live music on various Sundays and a mussel evening every month. It was always busy, and I had many regular customers. I also organized a Greek evening once. Duo Stratos came to perform, and of course I sang a few Greek songs with them. Everyone was enthusiastic. At the end of the evening, Stratos asked me if I wanted to perform with them, and as if I wasn't busy enough, I accepted the invitation. I missed performing and singing, so I couldn't turn down this offer. I had to find someone who could fill in for me on the evenings when I had a gig with Stratos. Jan didn't always have time either, because he was also very busy. His handyman business had turned into a paving company with employees. I loved performing with Duo (now Trio) Stratos in Greek restaurants, although it all became a bit too much for me. I wasn't getting much sleep anymore. I also didn't see Jan much anymore and I felt that it wasn't good for our marriage. I had to make choices, and that's what I did. We lived in the north of Leeuwarden and Jan's work was more in the west of the country, so we commuted every day. I suggested moving west and leaving Leeuwarden behind. Jan thought it was a good idea, so we looked for a buyer for our house, said goodbye to the café, and moved to Alkmaar, a beautiful cheese town in the north-west of the Netherlands.

The New Life in Alkmaar

CHAPTER 17

WE REALLY LIKED our new life in Alkmaar. We had found a beautiful corner house with a large garden just outside the city center, on a canal. Boats sailed by all day long, and I loved it. We also lived not far from the beach, and on Sundays we often went for a walk on the beach, followed by coffee and liqueur. Lovely. By then I had another dog, Pascha, a Yorkshire Terrier that Jan had given me as a gift. Pascha also loved the beach.

I was now 34 years old and I was starting to think more and more about motherhood. My biological clock was ticking and now that I had a family, the desire to be a mother was growing. I wasn't using contraception but hadn't gotten pregnant yet, and I was a little worried about it. I really wanted something of my own, especially since I never knew my parents. I did not get pregnant and decided to visit a doctor. It is often said that they take children, but nothing could be further from the truth. You get children; you do not take them. That was the beginning of a long journey of testing and even more testing. Fluid through my fallopian tubes to see if they were open. temperatures, pills, how quickly the sperm swam. Intercourse became clinical because it had to be done at predetermined times. All with the goal of getting pregnant. I really wanted to get pregnant and it just didn't work. I really wanted a child, something of my own. I had a laparoscopic surgery. The doctor asked about my past because he could see during that operation that I had been sexually abused and that could be the problem. I was put on the waiting list for IVF (In Vitro Fertilization), also known as test tube fertilization, something that was still in its infancy at that time. The wait was long, it was now 1991 and one could not say when the procedure would start. The waiting tested my patience but the thought that I might become a mother was amazing to me. I fantasized endlessly.

I filled my time, while I was waiting for that one phone call, with fun activities. I had stopped performing with Stratos because they had returned to their island Lesbos. I also stopped teaching for a while. I was handling the complete bookkeeping and payroll administration of our paving company. I also started working part-time at a daily newspaper advertising department.

It was 1992 and still no phone call for the start of my IVF treatment. I recorded a CD with Greek music with two Greek musicians. They can be listened to on YouTube. I also signed up for the Soundmix show with a Greek song by Melina Mercouri 'Milisse mou'. I made it through the preliminaries and was allowed to go to the final round. I didn't make it there. I participated in various television programs and had appearances in several series. I did everything to kill my waiting time. In the winters, I could be found in Tunisia where I performed with musicians at the hotel 'El Hana Beach' in Sousse. I quit my job at the newspaper because I found it hard to sit inside all day. I needed to be free, to breathe. I was restless because I wasn't receiving any calls from the hospital. The clock was ticking and I really wanted to become a mother.

Bad News

CHAPTER 18

TIME PASSED AND I still had not started the IVF treatment. It drove me crazy. In April 1993, I decided to go to Kalymnos (Greece) for a week. I wanted to be alone for a while and think about the future that for me consisted of becoming a mother to my child. I also wanted to reflect on my past and how I could find answers to the questions that were still on my mind. I wanted to answer before I became a mother, to close something for a new beginning.

It was wonderful on Kalymnos, a small island where people dove for sponges. I enjoyed the tranquility and nature. April was the pre-season, so there were no tourists yet. There wasn't much open, and when I was looking for a restaurant that was open one evening, I walked past a lovely little house where an older man was working in the garden. I stopped to ask him where I could find a restaurant to get a bite to eat. He told me that there was nothing open nearby but invited me to come inside. When I entered the cottage, I saw his wife and daughter threading grape leaves at the kitchen table. The wife and daughter were very friendly, and immediately drinks and a bottle of wine were placed on the table. The woman immediately started cooking because I had to eat, no matter what. Refusal was not an option. I discussed politics and such with the old man, and it turned into a wonderful evening. So friendly and so hospitable. I only left this lovely family's cottage around midnight after I had thanked them extensively for their hospitality.

Every day I would go to the beach for a couple of hours to swim and get some color. For a few days, I had noticed that I was getting red bumps on my face that looked very strange and inflamed. They became thicker and darker red every day. I also noticed that after a few hours in the sun, the bumps got worse. When the week was over, I returned to the Netherlands and when Jan picked me up from the airport, he was shocked. It looked like I had measles, but only on my cheeks. I also didn't feel very well at all and even though I had been on vacation, I was deadly tired, very strange. I decided to make an appointment with my doctor right away. He didn't trust it either and referred me to a dermatologist. I could get an appointment there fairly quickly, and the dermatologist scraped a small part for a biopsy. A week later, I had to come back for the results. The result was not good. He told me that I had Lupus, a disease I had never heard of before. Officially SLE or Systemic Lupus Erythematosus, an autoimmune disease that can occur in various organs. With me now, in the basal layer of the epidermis and in the underlying connective tissue. The main symptoms are fever, joint swelling, liver and kidney abnormalities. Treatment with corticosteroids usually provides temporary success. A large portion of patients with Lupus (mostly women) experience irreversible kidney damage that often leads to death. I was shocked by all the information about lupus and understood that this was a serious disease and that there was no cure for it. I had many questions, such as why I had developed this disease and how it would affect a possible pregnancy. Was it hereditary? I learned that only 1 in 10,000 people suffered from lupus and that it mostly affected women. I also learned that many women with lupus often miscarried in the eighth month of pregnancy and that lupus was also hereditary. I had many questions, but even the doctors did not have all the answers. Research was conducted, but because it is not a 'popular' disease like cancer, research was put on the back burner. I sought a physician who was knowledgeable about lupus and found one in Rotterdam, Dr. Swaak.

This physician had been conducting research for 25 years, and I trusted him. He accepted me as a patient and prescribed numerous medications. Plaquenil, Zyrtec, Arthrotec, Cortisone, etc. My life would never be the same again because I had to live with this new enemy in my body that was attacking my own body. Normally, your immune system defends you against enemies, but in this case, my immune system became my enemy and attacked me. Lupus cannot be cured because we still do not know why the immune system attacks its own body cells. I realized all too well that this would have a major impact on my life and that I needed to hurry up with certain things in my life. At the top of my agenda was: The truth about my parents.

I decided to place an advertisement in a widely read women's magazine called 'Libelle'. My appeal appeared in issue no. 28 of the magazine in July 1993.

I hardly knew my parents and I have no contact with their distant relatives. Does anyone know anything about J.H. Kerkhof and G.F. Kerkhof-Geertsema? Until around 1958, they lived at Oudezijl 11 in Nieuweschans. Any information is welcome.

I waited, and the first step was taken.

The Answers to My Questions

MY APPEAL WAS posted and, to be honest, I didn't expect much from it. However, I was very wrong because I received many letters. Many people wanted to help me and answer my questions.

There was a letter from the neighbor who had taken us in for the first three weeks, Mrs. Bisschop. There was also a letter from a Mr. de Jong, who wrote:

Dear Ms. Meijer-Kerkhof,

My wife recently came across your appeal for information about your family in Libelle magazine. From 1 June 1945 to August 1964, my father was mayor and secretary of the municipality of Nieuweschans, and after finishing school and completing my military service, I started working as a trainee civil servant in March 1950. This would enable me to provide you with some information, but it is of such a nature that I think it would be better to give it to you in person. After all, there is a reason why you hardly knew your parents. If you would like to meet me in person, please let me know.

Kind regards,
P.J. de Jong.

Another letter from Mrs van Dijk.

Dear Ms J.A. Meijer,

I happened to read your request for information about your parents. Your mother is from Bellingwolde and her youngest sister was my school friend. We lived close to each other, so I often visited your grandparents. I often met your mother there, as well as an older sister. After my marriage, I lived in Nieuweschans, where your mother also lived. She was married to Jan Kerkhof. If you would like further information, I can help you with that.

Many letters arrived, but one stood out. Mr. Smook's letter contained seven pages and told the whole story I had been searching for so many years.

Dear Ms Meijer (Janet),

A look back at the past. From 1940 to 1970, I lived on Oudezijl, about 100 metres away from your step-grandfather Tunnis Kerkhof. The old man lived there with his son Jan, your stepfather. Jan was still single in my youth, never went out and therefore had no regular friends and certainly no girlfriend. He never went to a bar either. Mother Kerkhof died early. Jan Kerkhof was known as a craftsman. He was a bench worker at the RAWI factories in Winschoten.

In fact, all the Kerkhofs were skilled craftsmen. Then Jan came home with a girl. The whole neighbourhood was stunned because Jan was dating, even though everyone knew that Jan was not a real man, he was infertile. The girl came from Bellingwolde and her name was Gezina (Sientje) Geertsema. As far as I know, this was in 1948. Your step-grandfather took a back seat when she arrived, because she quickly became the boss in the house. Then your stepsister Gerdina is born and it becomes clear that your mother has multiple relationships. Then your other stepsister is born, but your mother does not change her lifestyle. She meets a German truck driver and this man, whom I do not know, visits her several times during the day when your stepfather is at work. Then your step-grandfather rebels, but your mother does not want to be disturbed, so your grandfather is sidelined by being locked up in the attic. At one point, your mother starts travelling with the German truck, sometimes for several days at a time, leaving your stepsisters behind. Now comes the moment when the people of Oudezijl began to rebel against your mother. Firstly, because your old grandfather was locked up for several hours, but mainly because she left the children alone. The fact that she was unfaithful was understandable because your stepfather was not sexually satisfying. He was a good man, but he lacked passion. He would never hurt anyone. If you hit him, he would still say thank you. Even your birth in 1956 did not change your mother's lifestyle. Her hunger for sex continued to drive her. She was not a bad person, don't get me wrong.

Your mother was an active woman and did not fit in with your stepfather at all. She was also looking for love and warmth, which she did not get from your stepfather. He couldn't give her what she needed.

The day in 1958 comes back to my memory. It is around six o'clock in the afternoon on a weekday. Together with my co-driver, I walk from the garage on my way home. When we passed your house, we heard children shouting. Unsuspecting, we walked ontowards home. I just sat down at the table for dinner and the neighbor appears at the window and shouts: "Jan has stabbed Sientje." No longer thinking about food, I walk out of the house and am on my way to your house. After a while, two police officers appear on the sidecar. The local police are already in your home. After a quarter of an hour, the motorcycle officers come outside with your stepfather in the middle. Jan Kerkhof walks unshackled and with a dragging gait, his head deeply bowed. He briefly lifts his head and looks at us, probably asking for understanding, or perhaps he doesn't even see us. Later that evening, the truth comes out. Your stepsister Gerdina would have told the neighbors.

The fatal moment:

Jan Kerkhof is coming home from his job in Winschoten on the half-past five train. Your mother has presumably been out because she hasn't prepared any warm food. The whole family is in the kitchen, and Jan asks your mother why the food is not ready. Your mother provides an answer that must have angered your stepfather. She also refuses to prepare any food. Your stepfather accepts the situation again, gets up from his chair, takes bread and toppings and a bread knife, and walks to the counter. At the moment he is cutting the bread or wants to cut it, your mother makes a remark towards your stepfather. This one remark strikes Jan Kerkhof so deeply that even he, the sheep, becomes extremely angry and what no one could have suspected, not even your mother, happened at that moment. In all his frustrations and the many humiliations he has had to deal with over the years, that fatal moment came. Jan turns around and without a sense of direction he throws the knife away with all his strength and impotence. The knife Janet happens to hit your mother right in her heart and she must have died almost instantly. Your stepsisters were witnesses to the event and their screams reached me as previously described. I can well imagine that these women absolutely do not want to go back to that day in 1958 in any way. From your mother's family, I can also imagine that they do not want to be reminded of this period. I understand from you Janet that you want to know exactly how it was, which is why I called you directly.

Your stepfather took his life just before he was set to return to Nieuweschans. He also couldn't cope with that situation. Searching for and finding your real father will be a heavy task. You will have to search across the border. Good luck in any case.

I would gladly point out your mother's grave to you.

Regards, E. Smook.

Intense but also a clear letter. There were many letters and I decided to make an appointment with certain people to meet them and to be able to talk with them.

Finally See My Mother's Grave

CHAPTER 20

MANY PEOPLE WANTED to meet me, people who had known my mother and stepfather. It's sad that I only found my mother's grave when I was 37. I went to make appointments with letter writers and tried to spread them over two days. Jan naturally came along with me because he didn't want me to do this alone. Now the moment had come, after all those years, that I would get closer to the truth, and as a climax, I would visit my mother's grave. I had often searched for it but could never find it. I knew that in order to look ahead, I first needed to come to terms with the past. The first appointment was with a lady who had been a friend of my mother. At that time, she worked in the supermarket in Nieuweschans. When we arrived, the coffee was already ready. She described my mother's character in a kind way and there were no bad words from her mouth. She also explained why my mother did the things she did. That her own father sent her to the Germans' camp. She had sex there in exchange for his coffee and tobacco. Slowly, I began to get a picture of my mother. The second appointment was with Mrs. Bisschop, the neighbor who had taken us in for the first three weeks. We were going to have lunch with her. She still lived in the same little house while the house where I was born was no longer standing. It had been demolished. She also spoke lovingly about my mother and stepfather. At one point, she walked to a cabinet and came back with a small copper stove. She gave it to me as a gift and told me that my stepfather had made that stove in prison. A little work of art, and I was very happy with this gift. The third appointment was with the Smook family, who had written the extensive letter. After chatting for a while, the moment came to go to my mother's grave. I was nervous because I had been looking forward to this for a long time. At the cemetery, we followed Mr. Smook, and after walking for a short while, he stopped by a tree. Next to the tree was a bare patch of dirt and nothing else. I didn't understand it. Then he said: "Here lies your mother buried." He had a map in his hands, so it couldn't be wrong. There was absolutely nothing. No name, no stone, no flower… nothing. I was devastated. Was everyone so happy that she was dead and had dumped her in a hole in the ground? Did her parents and sisters hate her so much? I still bury my dogs more neatly and with more respect. I cried. I cried for my mother. I cried for her because I could feel her pain and sorrow. In the letter from Mr. Smook, he writes that her family does not wish to be reminded of that period, but they could have at least given her a respectful burial with at least her name on the grave. She was dumped as if she had never existed. They dumped her three children in an orphanage as if they also did not exist. What horrible people I never, ever want to meet in my life. SHAME ON THEM!!!

I had brought flowers and placed them at her grave. Then we left, and I was very sad.

The next appointment would make me even sadder. This appointment was with Mr. Buma. This gentleman had also written to me. He was a police officer in Nieuweschans in 1958 and had led the entire investigation. He told me that after what happened, an autopsy had of course been performed on my mother's body and during that autopsy the pathologist made a surprising discovery. It turned out that my mother was full of cancer. Cervical cancer to be precise and she wouldn't have lived long if she hadn't been killed. This was the second shock for me that day. All sorts of things were racing through my mind. Had that whole tragedy been for nothing? All those lives ruined for nothing? My stepfather in prison because he killed her when she might have died a natural death a month later? Life can be so strange.

We stayed talking for a while longer and then I wanted to go home. My head was full and I had a terrible headache. I didn't say much on the way. Finally, I knew the truth but it was so different from what I had expected. I was sad but even more angry. Angry at my grandparents, angry at my aunts. I hated them for how they treated my mother and her children. I hated those people and I still do to this day. It had been a very eventful day and I needed time to let everything sink in. A few days later, I called a professor, Mr. Burema. He was now working in Rotterdam, but in 1956 he worked in Nieuweschans as a doctor. He had helped bring me into this world at my birth and remembered my mother very well.

Everything in the puzzle was almost complete and I started to make sense of it so that I could move on with my life. I would like to know who my father was, but I am afraid I will never find out. That remains a dark void. My suspicion, my intuition tells me that he must have been a Greek truck driver. I have been living in Crete for more than 25 years at the time of this writing and I feel completely at home here, but will never know.

NOTE:

I cannot see you with my eyes nor can I touch you with my hands, but I will feel you in my heart. Forever you are my mother!

Present and Future

CHAPTER 21

Surviving (The Only Option!)

AFTER ALL THOSE years, I finally knew the truth about my past and had to accept it and make peace with it. I wanted to focus on the future now. I was still waiting for the call to start the IVF treatment. Now more than ever, I wanted something of my own. My own flesh and blood. My stepsisters both had young children, one had two children and the other three. I had no bond with them, especially after my search. My aunts were very angry about that, as were my stepsisters.

In the winter, I regularly went to Tunisia, to sing of course, but I also set up a new business. Jan and I were at the flea market every weekend with second-hand goods. I also designed bags and wallets myself that were made in a leather factory in Tunisia. I sold them at the flea market and to stores in the Netherlands. 'Habibi Leather Goods'. I was also regularly asked to perform at 'De Bastille' in Amsterdam and in 1994 I even had a performance at 'Paradiso', the pop temple in Amsterdam. I undertook everything to make waiting for the IVF more bearable. My creative brain was working overtime.

In June 1994, the long-awaited phone call finally came. I was allowed to start with the IVF. I had to go to the hospital to discuss the entire program with Doctor Roex, my gynecologist. I had to tell him also that I suffered from Lupus but I still wanted to give it a try.

I asked my neighbor and friend Inge to go with me to the hospital because she needed to learn how to give me injections every day. If she could do this, then I wouldn't have to go back and forth to the hospital every day for these injections. These injections were necessary to help as many eggs grow as possible. Inge first practiced at home on a cushion and later on an orange, and we had a lot of fun with that. After two weeks of injections, I had to go to the hospital for an ultrasound, and it turned out that the eggs were growing well. The injections turned my ovaries into a real chicken coop. As many eggs had to grow as possible. Inge also learned how to inject Humegon into me and she emerged as a good nurse. I often felt nauseous from the injections and suffered a lot from headaches. After a few days of Humegon, I started bleeding and in panic, I called the hospital because this couldn't be good. They did blood tests and on July 14th, they were going to do an ultrasound again. On the ultrasound, the growing eggs were visible; three eggs on the left side and four eggs on the right side. The next day back to the hospital to give blood for embryo creation. I experienced stomach pains and felt just like a plump chicken. On July 20th, back to the hospital for an ultrasound and blood tests. They already saw ten eggs then. The puncture of the eggs was scheduled to take place on Friday the 22nd. Inge was allowed to administer a special injection the night before, which would cause the ovulation to occur in 35 hours, enabling them to retrieve all the eggs. That Friday it finally happened. Inge drove me to the hospital. I could barely sit without pain in my lower abdomen because of all those eggs. In total, they managed to get sixteen eggs out. Jan would later come to the hospital with Sjaak (Inge's husband) because they had to transport the eggs in a cooler to another hospital in Amsterdam where they would grow the embryos. In the operating room, all the eggs were sucked from my fallopian tubes with a long needle and without anesthesia and this was the vilest pain I had felt so far. When all sixteen eggs were out and I was wheeled to a room on a bed, Inge was already waiting for me. Later she told me that she was very shocked because my skin color was gray from the pain. Jan and Sjaak set off to Amsterdam to deliver the cooler to the hospital there, where they would mix the eggs with the sperm cells in order to create embryos. Of the sixteen eggs, nine were usable. They had taken my lupus in account, and as a precaution, they had cultivated a portion of the eggs and sperm in my own blood and another half in donor blood. Fortunately, no embryos developed in my own blood, but they did in the donor blood. They had taken my lupus into account, and as a precaution, they had cultivated a portion of the eggs and sperm in my own blood and another half in donor blood. Fortunately, no embryos developed in my own blood, but they did in the donor blood.

On Friday, the 5th of August, I noticed that my temperature had dropped by two-tenths of a degree, and I knew that this was not a good sign. Around ten o'clock that morning, I experienced severe abdominal pain, and an hour later my whole world fell apart. I bled heavily, and I knew that everything had been for nothing; I was back to square one and felt hopeless and sad.

No one could understand how I felt. I also knew that this was my only chance to get pregnant because the lupus was in the way. I was allowed to try one more time, but I didn't see the point. My body would reject it again. Psychologically, I couldn't handle all of that, nor physically. This was it and I had to accept that I would never become a mother, that I would never be able to hold anything of my own flesh and blood, but I struggled with that a lot. I felt alone and misunderstood. I wanted another body, I wanted a child, something of my own but life apparently had other plans for me. Again I was tested so much and it hurt, terribly hurt.

The lupus worsened and attacked my body partly due to all the hormones I had been given. Doctor Swaak wanted me to take Prednisone, but I refused. He knew I was stubborn and respected me for the fact that I was fighting against my illness. I did not want to give in to the disease despite the fact that lupus is an incurable disease but I was determined to win. Nothing could bring me down, not even that damn disease! Jan was often angry with me because he felt that I wasn't taking care of myself and said that I was not accepting my illness, that I was in denial. Maybe he was right, but I knew that if I gave in, I would be lost. I have fought my whole life, and now was not the time or the moment to give up. I had learned in my life to fight and that is what I would continue to do. I wanted to live.

Accept and Move On

CHAPTER 22

OF COURSE, I had no choice but to continue my life even if it meant a life without children but with an illness. The sad thing is that most people do not know what lupus is and when you tell them that you have lupus they look at you in surprise and then say: 'but you look so good.' As if you are just making it up. You can't see it on the outside like a broken leg, and so you come across as unconvincing. I always try to give a brief explanation when asked.

What is lupus (SLE)?

When you have SLE, your immune system is working overtime. When your body detects a virus, the immune system goes after it to neutralize and eliminate the virus. My immune system does that too, but it doesn't stop once the virus has been dealt with. In fact, it continues to fight and attacks my own organs. This can be any organ in the body. Medication such as Plaquenil puts your immune system on low activity so it can cause less damage, but this also means that you are more susceptible because your immune defense is not fully effective anymore.

I often wonder how long it will take before SLE becomes a popular disease like cancer and AIDS, so that more money can be allocated for research into its causes, so that one day, perhaps soon, the often fatal disease SLE will be nothing more than a bad memory. Slowly I threw myself back into my work; the administration of our company, my leather goods from Tunisia, and the black market on the weekends. Regularly, I flew to Tunisia to manage everything there as well. They were very lazy there and, for example, stitched a blue zipper into a brown bag because the brown zippers were out. So I had to show my face there regularly. I also translated articles from French for the SLE patient association, which were then published in the monthly magazine. I had enough on my plate.

Our paving company was not performing well. The reason was that we had grown too quickly. We had also experienced a few harsh winters, which meant that we could not work but still had to continue paying our staff. I attempted to secure a loan from various banks, which I eventually succeeded in doing. This allowed us to continue for a while, but we had to remain cautious.

I still wasn't feeling well because the disappointment of the failed IVF was difficult for me to process. I hid it from the outside world, but inside it gnawed at me and hurt. Over the past two years, I had been through a lot, and of course, this had affected me. I was struggling with many things. I am a strong person, but I am not made of stone. I went about my work like a robot, but I was anything but happy. Jan and I were also living somewhat separate lives, and I had little support from him during that period. Perhaps it is different for men; I don't know. I think we both processed it in our own way.

Sonja

CHAPTER 23

IN FEBRUARY **1995,** I was back in Tunisia to sing and for my leather goods. I always loved being there, especially in winter because I hate the cold. One day, I was walking on the beach in Sousse when I saw some boys walking towards me with a small dog in their arms, a puppy. They walked straight up to me, handed me the puppy and ran away. There I was, holding a beautiful little white dog in my arms. I took him to my hotel room, even though dogs weren't officially allowed there. Since I knew the hotel manager, Mr. Ben Abdallah, well, I decided to have a chat with him. I explained the situation to him and he gave me permission to keep the puppy in the room until my departure. I named the puppy Habibi and immediately put him in the shower. I wanted to take him with me to the Netherlands, secretly in my shoulder bag. The hotel cleaners didn't want to clean my room anymore because of the puppy, but I understood that and didn't mind. They left clean towels outside my door in the hallway every day. I was fine with all of that. Habibi came with me to the Netherlands and would have a good life. In the end, Habibi didn't stay with us because he didn't get along well with my three Yorkshire Terriers. I found him a good home and made sure he was well cared for. In November, I went back to Tunisia and one morning I walked into a telephone office across from the hotel to call the Netherlands. There was a small baby lying on a bench. I looked around and searched for the mother of this child. She was standing in a telephone booth making a call. The baby was about a year old and was a girl. She had the sweetest smile you can imagine. What a darling. The mother finished her call and stepped out of the booth. I walked into the booth to start my phone call to the Netherlands. When I was done, I saw that the mother was still there with the child in her arms. The mother started talking to me in French and asked me if I would like to have a coffee with her somewhere because she wanted to talk to me. I had no problem with this, so we left the office together and looked for a terrace to have coffee. I had no idea what she wanted from me, but I waited to hear what she had to say. When we sat down on the terrace, I ordered coffee for both of us and she put the baby on my lap. She asked if I would give the baby a drink and handed me the bottle. The mother introduced herself as Miriam and the baby was her daughter Sonja. She said she was not married and that the child was the son of a Belgian truck driver she had had a relationship with. This driver worked for the MAES company,

Jeannette Meijer

a company I was familiar with. Her family had disowned her, she said, and she had not seen the Belgian man since. I was a little confused by her story because I didn't understand why she was telling me all this. What did she want from me? Maybe money? What was I supposed to do with that?

It soon became clear. Miriam wanted to get rid of the baby and she wanted me to take the baby to the Netherlands. She wanted me to adopt Sonja. I was in shock and upset. All kinds of thoughts were going through my head. Taking a dog to the Netherlands is one thing, but a baby? I was completely bewildered and didn't know what to make of the whole situation. Was I really sitting here drinking coffee with a woman who was offering me her baby? Was this real or was I dreaming? I wanted a baby so badly, but it didn't work out, and now I was being offered one? I didn't know what to make of the whole situation.

What kind of games was life playing with me? Of course, I wanted to take this sweet little girl home with me because then all my prayers would have been answered, even though she wasn't my own flesh and blood, but hey, we're talking about a child who, just like me, has been abandoned. I pulled myself together and told Miriam that I needed to think about it first. I invited her to come by the next morning to have breakfast with me at the hotel, and then we would talk further. I needed time to think about this whole situation. It was no small matter and I was still processing my failed IVF attempt. This woman and this situation reopened all my wounds. In half an hour, my world was turned upside down again.

The next morning, Miriam came to the hotel breakfast room with Sonja to have breakfast with me. I told her that I was married and that I wanted to discuss the matter with my husband first. Of course, he also had a say in this. I also wanted to find out in the Netherlands whether adoption was a possibility and whether it could be done legally. I asked her for a phone number and she gave me the number of her brother who lived in Tunis. I was to contact him. She also gave me a beautiful photo of Sonja with a message written on the back: 'You will be my new mummy.' I was moved and a plan slowly formed in my head. I had hope again. Miriam had given me hope again. I went back to the Netherlands the next day and discussed with Jan what had happened to me upon my return home. I also talked about it with friends, and everyone said I should go for it. Maybe it was meant to be. I made a decision and contacted Miriam's brother in Tunis. He knew of my existence and said that I should just come to Tunis to arrange everything. Friends contributed to the trip and also gave money for a lawyer, papers, etc. Everyone wished me success. In principle, I would go for 10 days to talk to the brother and to arrange a lawyer for the adoption. Overall, I had a plan in my head to take Sonja to the Netherlands, legally or illegally. I didn't care. I wanted this little girl.

I departed on the first of December to the city of Tunis where I had booked a hotel, and on the same day of my arrival, I called my brother for an initial meeting. We had no time to lose because there was much to arrange. He would come to my hotel the next day because unfortunately, he could not come on the evening of my arrival. The next afternoon he came, and we discussed the matter. I had brought some clothes for Sonja and some toys, which I gave to him. He said he would drive to Sousse in the evening to pick up various papers. (as if he couldn't have done that earlier). He asked me for money for the gas, and my irritation was triggered, but I didn't show it. I gave him some money, and we agreed to meet the following evening because he would be back from Sousse then. He suggested going out for dinner the next evening because he knew a good restaurant. I had a gut feeling and was not happy about it, which usually meant bad news. The next evening he picked me up from my hotel with his car and we drove towards the restaurant. I was tense because everything was moving so slowly and there was absolutely no progress. In the restaurant, he ordered a bottle of red wine, and while we were waiting for our ordered food, I asked him how it had gone in Sousse and whether he now had all the necessary papers so that we could visit the lawyer the next day. His answer to that made me feel even worse than I already did. He said: "Why do you want to adopt Sonja when we can also make beautiful babies together?" You understand that I felt extremely uncomfortable but didn't show it. I replied: "I know that but I have fallen in love with little Sonja." We ate and he told me that he worked in an office in the hospital in Tunis. He ordered a second bottle of wine which we drank and eventually, of course, he made me pay the bill. He took me back to the hotel but on the way he stopped and parked the car. He tried to make a move on me but I pushed him away and became incredibly angry. I told him I found him disrespectful and said that I wanted to keep it business-like. I asked him what time we were expected at the lawyer's the next morning, and he said he would pick me up at 10 am. Then he asked me for money again, and I refused. I got out of the car and walked back to my hotel. He drove away angrily.

Of course he didn't show up the next day and I decided to go look for him. He had written down the name of the hospital where he worked on a piece of paper (stupidly) and I also knew his last name, Mr. Chedri. So I knew enough to track him down and I would do that. The name of the hospital was written in Arabic and I couldn't read it but I wasn't born yesterday. I went to a little coffee shop and showed the note. The owner ordered a taxi for me, said where I wanted to go, and the taxi dropped me off neatly at the hospital. I began my search on the ground floor of the hospital. I asked everyone where I could find Mr. Chedri. First floor, second floor....I was on a mission and would not give up. Suddenly, I looked inside an office with an open door and there he was, sitting behind his desk. I stood in the doorway and called his name. There were more people at their desks, and when he saw me, he was incredibly startled and went pale. He quickly came over to talk to me in the hallway, away from the hearing of others. I was angry and asked why he hadn't shown up that morning. He said he had been called in to work, but that was an excuse. He said we would go the next day. Disappointed, I went back to my hotel. I had already been here for four days and this day was also a lost day. My money was spent on silly things and I was a bit done with it. I no longer believed him and didn't trust him anymore. I felt like he was playing a game with me. I decided to give him another chance, but the next day he didn't show up either, and I had had enough. I went to a travel agency and booked a round-trip ticket back to the Netherlands. I had been taken for a ride. They were only after my money and were playing games with my feelings. On my birthday, December sixth, I flew back to the Netherlands earlier than planned. Sad, disillusioned, richer in experience, poorer in illusion. If something seems too good to be true, it usually is not. Later, I reported the entire incident with names to the Tunisian Consulate in the hope that they would do something about it.

A New Way to Go

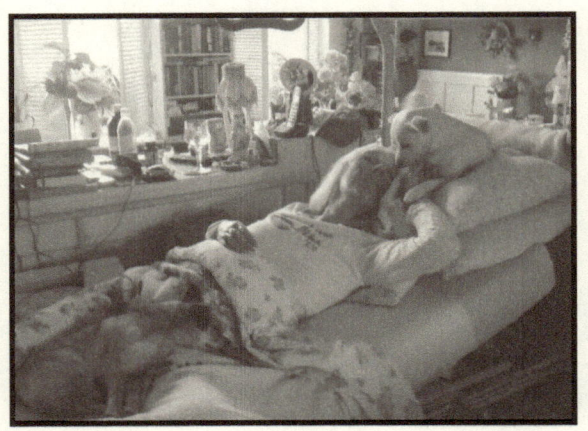

MY TRUST IN humanity had taken a heavy blow again, and I licked my wounds after returning from Tunis. I felt used, I felt silly, stupid, naive. What had I been thinking? How could I ever have thought that this would actually work? I had to finally accept that I would remain childless and that I would have to take another path because life is not waiting for the storm to pass. Living is dancing in the rain, and from now on, that is what I will do.

The paving company was doing worse, and in October 1996 we decided to file for our own bankruptcy before someone else would do it. This is always more favorable. In November 1996, I received a phone call one afternoon from a casting company where I was registered as a musician. That evening, the Moody Blues would perform live on a television show. They had made a comeback CD. They were going to perform the famous song "Nights in White Satin," which features a beautiful flute solo. However, the flutist had fallen ill and could not perform. The request was whether I would like to perform with the Moody Blues. Of course I wanted that. I didn't need to think about it for long. I received all the information and was expected in the studio on time.

Jan was outside in the garden building a small wall, and I told him about the phone call to play live on television with the Moody Blues. We quickly took a shower, got dressed, packed the flute, and set off for the studio, which was about an hour's drive away. In the car, I had time to listen to the cassette tape with the song I was going to play. Meanwhile, I was polishing my flute because it needed to shine, of course. Upon arriving at the studio, I received my own dressing room and practiced the flute solo a few times. Afterwards, I had a rehearsal on stage with the boys and then went to the canteen to eat something. Then I changed and went to the makeup room where they made me look nice and styled my hair. The performance went perfectly. From the Moody Blues, I received a signed double CD with the inscriptions: "Hope you had a great time, thanks" and "Thank you so much, you were great" signed by Justin Haywerd. I had enjoyed myself and was richer in experience again.

There followed years in which Jan and I were not completely on the same wavelength anymore. I had a lot to process, but Jan did too. His business went bankrupt, and he had to deal with that as well. He had to look for another job and found one. He started working as a truck driver, something he had done in the past. I could not continue with my leather goods business, firstly because I didn't want to go back to Tunisia after my experience with Sonja, but also because Jan went bankrupt and the tax authorities were going to take action against my business. We were married, and that's how it works. I started working at a postal company that handled the mail for travel agencies. It was nice work and only in the evenings. I also traveled a lot. I loved traveling, and it gave me a sense of freedom. France, Egypt, Turkey, and of course Crete.

In 1999 I had pain in my mouth and thick white spots appeared in my mouth. A biopsy was taken and it turned out to be leukoplakia. The precursor to mouth cancer. I was treated for it and this took a toll on my teeth.

In 2001, I decided in the spring to go work for a season in Crete. I had been there many times and my heart was and still is there. As I mentioned before, my feeling tells me that my biological father must have been a Greek. Perhaps a truck driver who worked in Germany or the Netherlands. At that time, many Greeks, Spaniards, and Portuguese worked in Northern Europe.

My intuition said it must have been a Greek. I quickly became proficient in the language, and my love for Greek music matches my character. In Greece, I feel at home. I belong there. I started working at the port of Hersonissos selling boat trips. One season there were several. In the winter I went back to the Netherlands for 4 months. Jan was happy for me and he also enjoyed his job as a truck driver. He wasn't home much either, of course, but slowly we found each other again. After working in the harbor for a few years, I was asked to be a guide on the Dotto train. This little train offered a four-hour tour, and we went into the mountains and visited the mountain villages where we also had lunch. Along the way, I described in 5 languages what people saw. Sometimes I went on jeep safaris with mentally challenged individuals. All in all, it was enjoyable work.

One day we stopped by train in a gorge and there were two ladies among the guests that day who caught my attention by the way they behaved. I was the guide and so I asked them if everything was okay. They were from the Netherlands and explained to me that they were both mediums. In the gorge, they received a lot of vibrations because during the war, the Germans and the Turks caused quite a bit of destruction there. I gave them a glass of raki and continued with my work. However, an idea was born in my mind. I wanted to sit with these two ladies during lunch so that I could perhaps ask them some questions about my mother. In the village of Afdou, we had lunch and I asked the ladies if I could join them, and they agreed. Then something incredible happened. Even before I could ask a question, one of the ladies said to me: "It's okay. Your mother is sitting next to you and she is so proud of you." I was in shock because we were complete strangers to each other. I had to swallow for a moment but was so happy with what this woman had said to me. I really wanted to hear this and after that, I didn't ask anything more. It was okay.

For eight months a year, I was working in Crete and four months in the winter in the Netherlands. I was now 55 years old and the lupus often got in my way. In 2011, I was walking with my thumb in a brace because there was an inflammation somewhere. I also woke up one morning and had no feeling in my toes in both feet. They felt dead. Very strange. I also started to experience severe back pain and decided to go back to the Netherlands in 2011 for some tests in the hospital. The joint in my thumb received a cortisone injection and got better. For my feet, I had to see a neurologist and after some tests, I was told it was polyneuropathy and that there was little they could do about it. The nerves in my feet were dead, probably because of my lupus. My back was also examined and initially, the neurologist suspected a hernia. After a year of injections for the pain, I decided to get a second opinion. No hernia. Two vertebrae were pressing against each other, which caused the pain. An Axialif surgery followed, during which they used a robot to secure the vertebrae with screws. I went into a plaster corset for a few weeks, and the back pain disappeared. They also placed marrow between the vertebrae obtained from my tail-bone in the hope that it would grow together. This all was done in 2012. Now that I was back in the Netherlands, I really missed Crete. My life was there, and I wanted to go back, but I decided to first write a book, an autobiography. I wanted to put my whole life on paper, for my own pro-cessing of it, but also to give other people the strength to keep going, no matter how difficult life can be. Especially the women and men who were sexually abused as children, I wanted to tell and show that you are not to blame and you must find the strength to move on as I found the strength to go on.

I did wright my Dutch book and it was published in 2015.

In 2015 abuse victims in youth care like myself, got until February 2017 to file a claim. The committee that received the claims said that it was touched by the devastating effect of the abuse on the lives of the victims.

I filed a complaint against the Dutch government that placed me in foster care without further care for me. Agencies that did not perform their work properly. They had to acknowledge it, and the Dutch govern-ment offered me their apologies and paid me a sum of money. That didn't make it right, but I did receive recognition.

Back to my Beloved Island, Crete

IN MY DUTCH book titled: "I was not allowed to be a child," I wrote my last page for Jan.

> To Jan, my buddy. For 27 years you have been my buddy through thick and thin. My rock in the surf. A buddy who knows me better than anyone else. You understood my fears, my doubts, and also my needs. You understood where I came from and why I did the things I did. You allowed me to stand next to you in freedom, without questions and without reproach.
>
> You supported me during my searches and you were always there when I was struggling because outsiders didn't understand me.
>
> You also held me back and told me several times that I no longer needed to prove myself, that it was time for me to believe in myself and accept myself.

When I wanted to go to Crete, for ten years in a row, you took me to the airport and 8 months later you picked me up again to then listen to all my adventures for four months.

I am very grateful to you for your unwavering support and understanding, and I hope that we will remain buddies until death do us part.

After my book was published and the Dutch government had acknowledged that they had been negligent, the nostalgia for Crete began to rise again in me. I discussed it with Jan and because Jan was almost at retirement age, he asked me if I would like it if he joined me on a trip to Crete. Of course I wanted that. That would be great. However, I wanted him to think it over once more because Jan was not much of a globetrotter and he loved our big garden in the Netherlands and the bees he kept. Crete was something completely different from what he was used to. However, he was sure about it and wanted to go to Crete. This meant that I had to take care of all the preparations. We had a house with three floors and many things had to be sold because we couldn't take everything with us. We needed to find a buyer for our very large garden, which had a shed and a greenhouse on it. I had a lot to do and asked some friends of mine in Crete to look for a cottage for Jan and me with a big garden because Jan needed to have something to do, of course. The plan was to return to Crete in August 2016 with the three dogs that I had brought from Crete. We packed three crates that would be shipped to Crete and we left. Our new little house was in Stalis, a village between Hersonissos and Malia. Slowly we started to furnish it. We bought a car. We had a large garden and worked in the garden every day. We built a nice, big chicken coop and got 50 chickens and a rooster. I sold the eggs to restaurants and friends. Life was good and Jan also enjoyed it and was happy in his retirement. I showed him the island and he was really fascinated. Now he understood all my stories, even the ones I had told him during the winter when I returned home about my life in Crete. We were happy. Then came the Corona time. A difficult time for everyone as everyone's life was turned upside down. Jan had a sore throat but never complained. For doctors, he was allergic. But when the sore throat persisted, I started to worry and I wanted him to go to a doctor with me. Just for reassurance. He was given three different antibiotics at the same time. However, this did not help and he was referred to an ear, nose, and throat doctor. The doctor examined him and looked very concerned but did not say much. He received different medications but I had a bad feeling and didn't trust it. I went back to the doctor alone and told him that I wanted to hear the truth. I wanted to hear that one word; I wouldn't leave until I did. Eventually, he uttered the word. Cancer. My suspicions were confirmed. It was March 2020 and I saw Jan deteriorating. He could hardly eat anymore because he could not swallow. In the hospital, he got a stoma in his throat and one in his stomach through which I had to pump the food. It was terrible to see him suffer like that. He could no longer speak, so he wrote everything down. He kept getting thinner no matter what fatty foods I pureed to give him some weight. On December 14, 2020, he passed away and was freed from his suffering. I sat next to him, holding his hand. When I realized it was over and that he was relieved from his suffering, I sat there, looking at him and I cried in silence. The little dogs were lying next to him on the bed. I was alone again and had lost my buddy. For 34 years, he had been my buddy through thick and thin. I stood up and poured myself a big glass of wine. I wasn't in a hurry, why would I be? It was around 9 pm. I had already spoken with the funeral director a month in advance and ordered a burial site that Jan had chosen himself. We had been living towards this moment. We knew it would come. I had another wine and then decided to take a walk with the dogs. I was actually very calm. I called the doctor and I called the undertaker. That same evening, Jan was taken out of the house because that happens fairly quickly here in Crete. The burial was two days later with only a handful of people because it was during corona times.

You are truly gone now,
your soul has found the way on its own.
I have seen your body off.
I cry and feel empty.
In the drizzling rain, I walk home.
Then someone asks me for directions,
I don't know, because for a moment
the only way I know
is the one you found.

It is now 2025 and I have been living without my buddy for four and a half years. I miss him very much, our deep conversations, his advice on certain matters. Of course, I can manage without him, but I miss him every day. I moved house because I couldn't stay in the house where he had been so ill for ten months. I am now retired myself and don't need to work anymore. Gives me more time to do the things I like to do like gardening, writing and my three dogs.

Life is good and has made me stronger. My positive outlook on life has always kept me going and made me stronger. For me, the glass is always half full rather than half empty. I am also convinced that everyone who comes into your life is either a blessing or a lesson. Both are positive.

To my family.

When your own family dumps you and they don't want to know you, it's hard to understand. The 'why' keeps running through your head and you wonder what you did wrong.

I have nothing good to say about their behavior in 1958 and the years that followed. I think they should be ashamed of the fact that they buried their sister or daughter in a hole in the ground just to get rid of her as quickly as possible. They didn't even bother to place a stone there with the names of her three daughters on it. They didn't even bother to be present when her body was "dumped". They haven't quite danced on her grave yet.

As for the three children who were left behind as orphans, including myself. I can only speak for myself in this case and will never be able to understand why they placed me in an orphanage without shame. They never looked back at me for the rest of my life. I did not ask for life and was not to blame. What were they so afraid of? Was it my misfortune that I was my mother's daughter and therefore unwanted? Was it my fault that there was no father in sight? I will never get an answer, but one thing is certain for me:

They should be ashamed of themselves!!!